THE NATIONAL

A GUIDE TO AMERICA'S

University of Nebraska Press ❧ Lincoln and London

GRASSLANDS

UNDISCOVERED TREASURES

By Francis Moul

Photography
by Georg Joutras

Publication of this book was made possible by
The Ronald K. and Judith M. Stolz Parks Publishing
Fund, established at the Nebraska Community
Foundation. Use of this fund for this purpose is
made in memory of Wayne Kemper Parks (1909–95)
and Hazel Virginia Hill Parks (1911–91), lifelong
Nebraskans who were born on Madison County
farms, married on March 19, 1930, and farmed in
Madison and Pierce counties.

Maps by Ezra Zeitler and Mat Dooley

Library of Congress Cataloging-in-Publication Data

Moul, Francis, 1940–
The national grasslands : a guide to America's
undiscovered treasures / Francis Moul; photography
by Georg Joutras.
p.   cm.
Includes bibliographical references and index.
ISBN-13: 978-0-8032-8320-6 (paperback : alk. paper)
ISBN-10: 0-8032-8320-2 (paperback : alk. paper)
1. Grasslands—West (U.S.) 2. Prairies—West (U.S.)
3. Grassland ecology—West (U.S.) 4. Prairie ecology
—West (U.S.) 5. Grassland conservation—West (U.S.)
6. Prairie conservation—West (U.S.) I. Title.
QH104.5.W4M68 2006
333.74'160973—dc22   2006003496

Designed and set in Minion by A. Shahan.

Cover: Pawnee Buttes, Pawnee National Grassland

Contents

List of Illustrations   vii
List of Maps   vii
Acknowledgments   ix
Prelude   1
Introduction   5

PART I.   The History of the National Grasslands   9
1.   "No Darker Chapter nor Greater Tragedy"   11
2.   Land, the First Essential   17
3.   A Strange and Dramatic Moment   23
4.   Broken-up Badlands, Thin Threads of Trees   37
5.   Highest Purpose of the Grasslands   45

PART II.   A Guide to the National Grasslands   55
An Abundance of Sage Hens   57
National Grasslands Visitor Center   58

Western States Grasslands 58

Crooked River National Grassland 58

Curlew National Grassland 60

Butte Valley National Grassland 63

Northern Great Plains Grasslands 67

Little Missouri National Grassland 67

Sheyenne River National Grassland 70

Cedar River National Grassland 73

Grand River National Grassland 75

Fort Pierre National Grassland 77

Buffalo Gap National Grassland 80

Oglala National Grassland 84

Thunder Basin National Grassland 87

Southern Great Plains Grasslands 91

Pawnee National Grassland 92

Comanche National Grassland 94

Cimarron National Grassland 97

Rita Blanca National Grassland 99

Kiowa National Grassland 101

Black Kettle National Grassland 103

McClellan Creek National Grassland 106

Caddo National Grassland 107

Lyndon B. Johnson National Grassland 109

Grasslands National Park of Canada 111

PART III. Bison Instead of Cattle? 115

Afterword 131

Photographer's Notes 135

Notes 139

Index 145

Illustrations

following page 2
1. Crooked River National Grassland
2. Curlew National Grassland

following page 18
3. Mount Shasta, Butte Valley National Grassland
4. A Swainson's hawk, Butte Valley National Grassland
5. Little Missouri National Grassland
6. Blister beetles, Little Missouri National Grassland

following page 34
7. Remnants of tallgrass prairie, Sheyenne River National Grassland
8. Cedar River National Grassland
9. Grand River National Grassland
10. Fort Pierre National Grassland
11. Abandoned farmstead, Buffalo Gap National Grassland
12. Toadstool Geologic Park, Oglala National Grassland
13. A passing storm, Oglala National Grassland
14. Sunset, Oglala National Grassland

following page 50
15. Passing coal trains, Thunder Basin National Grassland
16. The Pawnee Buttes, Pawnee National Grassland
17. Cow and passing storm, Pawnee National Grassland

following page 66
18. Comanche National Grassland
19. Indian pictograph, Comanche National Grassland
20. Cimarron National Grassland

following page 82
21. Rita Blanca National Grassland
22. Mills Canyon, Kiowa National Grassland

following page 98
23. Black Kettle Lake, Black Kettle National Grassland
24. McClellan Creek National Grassland

following page 114
25. Great egrets in tree, Caddo National Grassland
26. Garden coreopsis, Lyndon B. Johnson National Grassland

following page 130
27. Grasslands National Park of Canada
28. Prairie dogs on burrow, Grasslands National Park of Canada

Maps

Legend   56
1. National Grasslands   56
2. Crooked River National Grassland   59
3. Curlew National Grassland   61
4. Butte Valley National Grassland   64
5. Little Missouri National Grassland (North)   66
6. Little Missouri National Grassland (South)   68
7. Sheyenne River National Grassland   71
8. Cedar River National Grassland   73
9. Grand River National Grassland   75
10. Fort Pierre National Grassland   78
11. Buffalo Gap National Grassland   81
12. Oglala National Grassland   85
13. Thunder Basin National Grassland   88
14. Pawnee National Grassland   93
15. Comanche National Grassland   95
16. Cimarron National Grassland   98
17. Rita Blanca National Grassland   100
18. Kiowa National Grassland   102
19. Black Kettle National Grassland   105
20. McClellan Creek National Grassland   106
21. Caddo National Grassland   108
22. Lyndon B. Johnson National Grassland   110
23. Grasslands National Park of Canada   113

Acknowledgments

Francis Moul

This book would not have been possible without the gracious help of the people of the U.S. Forest Service, from the acting deputy chief to forest supervisors and district rangers, to so many fine professional staff people in the field. They were knowledgeable, patient, and answered many, many questions at length and with excellent information. Thank you.

Thanks also to the folks who agreed to read the text, as the chapters rolled off the computer, and make comments on content, style, grammar, and more. They caught some mistakes and helped me rethink some sections that needed it. Thanks, then, to John Wunder, Bob Wickersham, and Catherine Witt. Of course, as always, the final version is my own responsibility. Tyler Sutton and I spent many an hour over lunch in conversation about this work, and I appreciate his encouragement and contributions. South Dakota author and bison guru, Dan O'Brien, was also a lunch mate with talk about his work and was gracious to allow us to quote from his book, Buffalo for the Broken Heart. Thanks also to the Nebraska State Historical Society for allowing use of parts of an article I did for them in the Winter 1999 issue of Nebraska History, "The Biggest Partner: The Federal Government and Sioux County, Nebraska."

Paul Royster, former director of the University of Nebraska Press, saw the vision of a book about the national grasslands and gave us the initial go-ahead, and present director Gary Dunham has competently followed through with the production of the final work. Georg Joutras has been a marvelous photographer and terrific collaborator on this book. Two University of Nebraska–Lincoln graduate students in geography, Ezra Zeitler and Mat Dooley, produced the great maps of the National Grasslands.

Much of the research of and travel to the national grasslands was done during five years of study for a doctoral dissertation in environmental history. Throughout those times, and during the extra year's work on this book, my greatest supporter, critical guide, and helpmate in all phases has been my wife and best friend, Maxine.

I dedicate this book to Maxine, Jeff, Diane, and Adia Jennifer.

Georg Joutras

First off, let me just say that I am indebted to Francis Moul for his blind belief that I could get the kind of images to do his eloquent text proud. Little did I know the adventures that awaited me when Francis called me up and asked if I wanted to do a book on the national grasslands. (As I recall, my articulately worded reply was . . . "Sure.")

But that is the way things tend to work out for me. A call is taken or someone previously unknown walks into my gallery, a question is asked, I reply by gut reaction alone, and my life takes another interesting and always rewarding turn.

Thanks Francis.

I have spent fifteen months traveling and photographing twenty-one national grasslands (twenty in the United States, one in Canada) and along the way have seen incredible views, witnessed fascinating aspects of wildlife behavior, and met some wonderful people. In the next few paragraphs, I would like to thank those who made my travels more successful, greased the pathways of bureaucracy, or generally offered me a helping hand when most needed.

At the top of my list is Christy Cheyne at Butte Valley National Grassland in California. She unselfishly agreed to escort me around this wonderful area with very little advance notice, and on a holiday weekend to boot. Wow. This type of dedication is hard to find, and I am still in awe of her willingness to help someone she didn't really know by offering me the luxury of her time and knowledge. Along with Christy, I need to thank Chris Briggs, graduate student and hawk spotter extraordinaire, for his help during my visit.

Thanks to Richard Hill, Steve Kitrell, Chief Ranger Steve Currey, and Maggie Marstend at Pawnee National Grassland for allowing me to pick their collective brains and tag along on the swift fox survey, which proved that there really are swift fox out there among the seemingly empty prairies.

Jonathan Proctor, with the Predator Conservation Alliance, supported my efforts with information and timely advice and has helped "get the word out" about my images to a wider audience. Jonathan, along with his partners in crime, are doing good work, most of which occurs behind the scenes.

Others who offered assistance were Bob Hodorff and Doug Sargent at Buffalo Gap National Grassland, Albert Sanchez at the Lyndon B. Johnson National Grassland, Jimmy Hall at Kiowa and Rita Blanco Grasslands, Mike Lockhart with the Wyoming U.S. Fish and Wildlife Service, Sean Anglum and Ivey Brower at the Cheyenne Mountain Zoo in Colorado Springs, Colorado, and Colleen Oquist at Comanche National Grassland.

Thanks go to Mike Phillips, executive director of the Turner Endangered Species Fund, and to Tom and Irma LeFaive at the Turner Bad River Ranch in South Dakota. Kevin Honness at the Bad River Ranch deserves special recognition for his insight and for allowing me the freedom to capture swift fox images I am proud of.

I spent an enjoyable day at Dan O'Brien's Cheyenne River Ranch within the Buffalo Gap National Grassland. Thanks to Dan for allowing my visit, and special thanks and appreciation go out to ranch foreman Gervase Hittle who, along with Donna Galati, made my time among the bison so memorable.

Paul Royster, past director of the University of Nebraska Press, needs to be acknowledged for his belief in this project and the willingness to give it a green light. Thanks to current director Gary Dunham for his insights and help in shepherding forward this work toward publication.

And of course, I could not have completed this task without the love and support of my wife, Pamela, and daughter, Maddie.

So there you have it. My list of individuals who have touched this book in some way. I am positive I have inadvertently forgotten one or more people, and for that, I apologize in advance. Show mercy . . . on some days I barely know my own name.

THE NATIONAL GRASSLANDS

Prelude

The grasslands of the Great Plains were born from the mountains. Great mediterranean seas covered the vast interior lands time and again, joining the Arctic Ocean and the Gulf of Mexico, laying down hundreds of feet of sediment that eventually became the underlying sandstone, shale, and limestone beds of the Great Plains. Then the Rocky Mountains, slowly in inches per decade, thrust up in great chunks of granite to become the Shining Mountains and emptied the Bearpaw Sea. At the same time wind, rain, glaciers, and the soft touch of flowing water wore down the mountains until they were half their original size.

All those billions of tons of debris were rolled, crushed, and blown until they covered the inland basin, hundreds of feet thick. Volcanoes blew more tons of ash. Still the elements worked. Snow and glacier melt created huge roiling rivers that cut into the plains. When they dried up, the winds blew the sand and dirt eastward, to make unique features like the Nebraska Sand Hills, loess hills, and the plains. During the Ice Ages, glaciers rumbled over the plains, dragging boulders from Canada, carving out huge valleys and lakes, and turning the Missouri River away from Hudson Bay toward the Mississippi, creating together one of the longest rivers in the world.

About sixty-five million years ago, the last landlocked sea flowed out into the Gulf of Mexico, pushed out by the rising Rocky Mountains. For millions of years a subtropical environment developed with huge forests, marshes, and the beginnings of African-like savanna plains. Open grassland was home to long-legged grazing animals. There was a general drying period, from about eighteen million years ago, due in part to the rain shadow of the western mountains. Moist Pacific air dumped its water on the west slopes, with the dry air then sweeping onto the plains. Hardwood forests and tallgrass prairies gave way to vast reaches of shortgrass plains and small woods bordering rivers and streams.

Still, the wind and rain eroded the High Plains, tearing away rivulets of mud, leaving only buttes and ridges, escarpments of harder rock to show the phantom magnificence of the old plateaus. All the rest was an ocean of grass, rolling in seemingly endless waves across the horizon, dipping where glacial fingers dug trenches, flowing up hills left behind by the errant forces of erosion.

Now came the new animals of the Great Plains, today all extinct: tiny two-horned rhinoceroses, oreodons that resembled a cross between a sheep and a pig, and three-toed horses as small as dogs. Deer not much larger than a house cat shared space with camels that had very slender legs and long necks. One of the strangest animals was the chalicothere, a relative of both horses and rhinos. It had a horse's head, long front legs that sloped to short hind legs, and great curved claws for feet to dig up roots and tubers. One of the most dangerous animals was the "terrible pig," six feet tall with an over-large head and tusks as thick as a human's wrist. They were omnivores, equally at ease eating fruit or an animal carcass.

Over the millennia, drought came and wet cycles flourished, making the Great Plains expand east, then retract west, settling generally at the hundredth meridian. There, the land slopes up from two thousand feet to the foothills of the Rockies and the rain and snow seldom falls more than twenty inches a year. It is the semiarid land of short grasses, especially buffalo

1. The varied topography of the Crooked River National Grassland in Oregon includes flat plains, running streams, and hilly crags.

2. Curlew National Grassland, Idaho

grass—tender and nutritious in the greening spring, still hearty through the summer, and a good mouthful of food when it is winter-dried.

The mountains gave up their bulk, saw it spread out over the plains and then wash down to the ocean. They kept the rain and dried up the plains that were left over. But the plains became the home of teeming millions of animals that moved out over the grasslands in a pageant of life that must have seemed perfectly balanced between predator and grazer, life and death equaling out over the long years of fighting fang and hoof.

And then came people.

In a quick wink of geological time, modern humans rose up about one hundred thousand years ago, probably in Africa, breaking all the rules of nature. There was no thick fur to protect them against the sting of blowing snow and icy chills. No long, needlepoint fangs to rip the life out of prey. Humans could not outrun the fast grazers, could not fly away on the wind, or dive deep into the raging waters. Humans were puny in a world set against them.

But humans had an enlarged and complex brain. They had fingers and thumbs that could make weapons out of rocks and wood and cooking pots out of clay. They could talk and organize into bands of hunters and fishers and primitive farmers. They could imagine civilization, the vision we have of life in space, time, and mind. In time they conquered the world and everywhere altered that perfect balance of life that had lasted through the millennia, broken only by the catastrophes of the universe itself: asteroids plunging to earth.

Perhaps ninety thousand years ago, more or less, a broad plain reappeared and joined the steppes of Russia with the mountains of Alaskan lands as the Ice Age pulled so much water from the oceans that a new land emerged. Grass, the world's most restless plant, quickly spread across the thousand miles of the land called Beringia and drew the huge mastodons and many species of grazers and their predators south to a new land teeming with its own unique zoological stew. Humans eventually followed the migration and drifted down the long trail from the Siberian plains. They walked past the tall glaciers of Alaska and spread southward. A glacial advance left two huge ice sheets in Canada and Alaska, with a gap between them forming an ice-free corridor from Alaska down along the eastern edge of the Shining Mountains to the northern Great Plains. Those early travelers could look up to glacial ice cliffs more than a thousand feet tall.

The ice melted and refroze, opening and closing the corridor. The megafauna of large mammals adapted to the cool, moist climate of the glacial margins. Camels and horses, gigantic sloths, bison twice as tall as a man, and the elephantlike mastodons all mixed together, crossing back and forth over the land of the Bering Strait, followed by their most dangerous hunters, humans.

First came the big game hunters, warriors of untold courage who would attack mastodons with spears and primitive knives. Only by gathering into bands with brave leaders who could signal the best attack were they able to make a kill. In these small groups they found solitary animals, often chasing them into bogs or trapping them in gullies. In time, along with environmental and climate changes, the big game hunters probably hastened the mastodon extinction with their hunting, about thirteen thousand years ago. This left the small version of plains bison, descendant of the much larger ancient bison, as the predominant grazer of the Great Plains. It became the food basket and complete commissary of the tribes that came and went over the plains until about eight thousand years ago.

Then came the drought. Given the name of Altithermal, this became an interval of many decades, perhaps even centuries of warmer, drier climate. Tallgrass prairies that sustained mammoths, horses, and other grazers were gradually replaced by warm-weather short grasses and bison, which thrived on the new vegetation. The plains dried up to dusty swales and both people and their prey moved away. This long time of heat and aridity divided the ancient people from their modern descendants who came later to the plains.

Introduction

The 1930s in America—the Dirty Thirties—was a transforming decade, especially in the Great Plains, the one-fifth of the land that makes up its central heartland. There was severe drought and economic depression, the combination causing one of the greatest social disruptions in peacetime for the entire nation. National unemployment approached 50 percent and more, price deflation caused money to become extremely dear, and farmers destroyed livestock rather than lose money trucking animals to auction houses for pennies on the dollar in sales.

The federal partnership with American citizens changed enormously as President Franklin D. Roosevelt attempted to meet the new needs of a nation and its farm population faced with the loss of their land, bankruptcy, and even starvation in a dry, desiccated landscape. His New Deal programs initiated reforms in federal social, economic, and conservation policies, many of which remain in place today.

In dramatic moves, New Dealers ended the practice of giving public lands away or selling them very cheaply—a practice as old as the nation it-self—and reversed that to preserving the remaining federal lands and buy-ing back some 11.3 million acres of overgrazed, mismanaged rangeland and farmland across the nation. Out of those land purchases came today's na-tional grasslands, twenty reserves in the Great Plains and the West, totaling almost four million acres.

The national grasslands were the result of an unprecedented social revo-lution, paying distressed farm families for submarginal land that could no longer support them and attempting to resettle them in subsidized homes in small, new towns; on subsistence homesteads of twenty and forty acres; or in newly created "garden cities." However, like many New Deal ideas, this reform was hastily planned and executed and tragically underfunded. Originally, seventy-five million submarginal acres were identified for pur-chase, but bureaucratic shuffling, resistance from conservative members of Congress, and lack of funding cut the program back. The 11.3 million acres eventually purchased came under nine different federal agencies before fi-nally being dispersed to state and federal agencies and Indian reservations. The U.S. Forest Service, an agency of the U.S. Department of Agriculture (USDA), received about 3.8 million acres, and on June 20, 1960, they were designated as nineteen national grasslands. A twentieth national grassland was added in California in 1991.

From the very beginning, the national grasslands' concept has been a step-child within the USDA. They are most often managed along with national forests, which receive more attention, funding, and staff. Although there is excellent royalty income from oil, gas, and coal leases on some national grasslands, plus income from the sale of cattle grazing permits, that money goes into state, county, and federal treasuries and does not contribute to the operating budgets of the grasslands.

There have been continuing debates on correct grasslands management, whether for private grazing, public recreational use, wildlife preservation, or a combination of all these. About every ten to fifteen years, an extensive public process provides new management plans, and this planning has re-cently been completed for a number of grasslands. There is also a continu-ing debate over the charge per acre for grazing permits for ranchers, which are traditionally much lower than fees charged for private lands.

Under a 1960 mandate, the national grasslands are to be managed for outdoor recreation, range, timber, watershed protection, and wildlife and fish management purposes. They are all open for many public uses, such as hiking and camping, picnics, and "windshield tours" by visitors. They are marked with signs, and roads are open for public usage. Inexpensive but highly detailed maps are available at ranger stations. Best of all, there are no crowds on the national grasslands. Visitors are often alone in a seemingly infinite expanse of grass and sky where the solitude and beauty take time to assimilate.

The grasslands are largely undiscovered treasures of an important national heritage. Their recent history encompasses the exciting days of cattle drives from Texas and pioneer settlement on the plains. Their beauty is subtle but enchanting. The wildlife is extensive with hundreds of species of animals and plants, and there are constantly changing scenes as the seasons progress.

This book is presented in three parts. Part 1, the history of the national grasslands, begins with a look at drought on the Great Plains and in the West, how human intervention affected the land, and the early ideas to correct severe range problems of the 1930s. Next is a short history of land development in America including ideas on proper land use and state experiments on land utilization that foreshadowed the New Deal relief programs. An extensive and detailed history of the social, political, and economic revolution of the New Deal, leading directly to the designation of the national grasslands, is given in chapter 3. In chapter 4, a case study of how one grassland developed gives a detailed look at conditions in the 1930s, the land purchases, and the infrastructures that evolved. Chapter 5 discusses the challenges of restoring and managing the newly bought public lands and creating laws to guide their management as drought and the Depression were ending in the 1940s. Part 2 is a detailed description of terrain, wildlife, flora, public facilities, and important features of each grassland, including Grasslands National Park of Canada. Part 3 provides analysis of grassland issues, delivers conclusions about them, and presents future alternatives.

I. THE HISTORY OF THE NATIONAL GRASSLANDS

1. "No Darker Chapter nor Greater Tragedy"

The Pacific Ocean is enormous. It is also, since the Pleistocene Age, the blue-water force that determines whether drought or plentiful rains will embrace the Great Plains.

The cause of droughts on the Great Plains is specific and known, says geographer John Hudson. He explains that there are three air masses that converge on the plains, two causing precipitation while the third, from the Pacific, produces drought. He notes that "cold, dry air from the Canadian Arctic hugs the ground and lifts above it warm, moist air from the Gulf of Mexico to produce rain or snow." Pacific air, fairly mild, carries abundant water vapor, but that condenses against the mountain ranges west of the plains. As the Pacific air descends the east-front rainfall shadow of the Rockies, it is warm and dry, not likely to produce rainfall. Thus, Hudson says, when "the Pacific air stream dominates the mid-continent, day after day of dry conditions are the norm and the pattern can last enough to produce serious drought."[1] He might have added that hot, dry tropical air out of Mexico—instead of the moist Gulf winds—has the same results.

A prolonged lack of rain defines drought, and the Great Plains has seen plenty of that, as we know from observation and history as recorded in tree rings. According to one government report, drought occurs when "natural vegetation becomes desiccated or defoliates unseasonably and crops fail to mature owing to lack of precipitation, or when precipitation is insufficient to meet the needs of established human activities."[2] On the Great Plains, drought is "the most significant climatic element" in the environment, as "it determines the 'carrying capacity' of the region," according to one source.[3]

One of the earliest investigations of drought, a 750-year tree-ring study, starting at A.D. 1220, shows twenty-one droughts in western Nebraska, each exceeding 5 years, for an average of 12.8 years, with about a 24-year average interval between droughts. Eight of those episodes averaged 20.6 years and the granddaddy of them all lasted 38 years, from A.D. 1276 to 1313.[4] About eight thousand years ago, following the last Ice Age glacier on the Great Plains, increasing aridity caused an eastward and northward expansion of grassland, as the contemporary boreal forest shifted north. There was a "protracted warm dry interval."[5] That Altithermal climatic episode, with higher temperatures and reduced precipitation, lasted until about forty-five hundred years before the present time and pushed humans to adapt farming practices to supplement bison hunting. Maize was brought to the plains from Mexico and adapted to the harsh climate.

Although the ten-year drought of the 1930s is generally acknowledged as one of the most severe since European settlement of the plains, tree-ring studies show other droughts just as harsh. One study indicates that the 1860s were dryer than but not as hot as the 1930s, while low rainfall and hot weather were found in the 1620s, 1750s, and the first half of the nineteenth century. The 1620s episode matches the 1930s in severity.[6] Nonetheless, it was the great drought and economic depression of the 1930s that transformed American agriculture and brought about the social revolution of the New Deal that ultimately resulted in a network of national grassland reserves.

The history leading to that disaster is as familiar as a Western movie. Texas cattlemen and their cowboys trailed herds of longhorns to lush central plains grasslands immediately after the Civil War. The herds met the west-ward-reaching railheads, from Missouri to western Nebraska, for shipping to Chicago and the East Coast beef markets. As many, or more, cattle were moved into the northern plains of Wyoming, Montana, and the Dakotas, and eventually into the Nebraska Sand Hills, where huge ranches spread over public lands.

The inevitable struggle between later homesteading farmers and en-trenched ranchers using the public land for free sparked conflict, and in many areas the settlers won out, fencing their small 160-acre farms and plowing up the virgin prairie. The horrible winters of 1885–86 and 1886–87 with a huge die-out of entire free-range cattle herds changed ranching for-ever from the open range to enclosed pastures, winter hay feeding, and the crossbreeding of purebred cattle.

J. E. Weaver, a noted plains botanist and ecologist, describes what hap-pened next, as growing numbers of settlers broke the prairie. First, he wrote, they would plow up a small tract to grow enough winter feed to sustain their livestock, keeping the rest for pasture. "Frequently the cultivated fields were cropped for a number of years and then abandoned to return to native prairie."[7] The post–Civil War industrial revolution with its new labor-saving farm machinery stimulated more crop production with less manpower, and eventually the internal combustion engine powered tractors just in time for the great farm boom times and profits of World War I. "Immense areas that had previously been regarded as 'too risky' for growing wheat were broken for crop production. It was estimated that eighteen million acres were un-der cultivation."[8]

The war ended and boom prices plummeted. An agricultural depres-sion beat the 1929 stock market bust by several years and then came the 1930s drought. There was not enough rain for crops, so the demand grew for rangeland and the prairies were severely overgrazed. Weaver notes, "As cultivation continued despite the decreased rainfall, the soil became more pulverized, less porous, and more susceptible to erosion by both wind and water. Runoff was increased manifold and the rate of erosion was accelerat-ed enormously. . . . The year 1933 marked the beginning of a period of great desiccation in the mid-continental grasslands."[9] The winds blew across this dead land for eight years, starting in 1931, creating dust clouds thousands of feet tall, blowing Great Plains topsoil all the way to the decks of ships on the Atlantic Ocean and to London, Krakow, and Moscow.

"[T]he earth ran amok. And not once or twice, but over and over for the better part of a decade: day after day, year after year, of sand rattling against the window, of fine powder caking one's lips, of springtime turned to despair, of poverty eating into self-confidence," wrote historian Donald Worster.[10]

Surely there had been dust storms in those extended droughts of long ago, but these choking deluges of the '30s were "primarily the work of man. . . . The storms were mainly the result of stripping the landscape of its natural vegetation," Worster wrote.[11]

There were similar thoughts in the U.S. government. In an unusually hard-hitting report on the condition of 728 million acres in the West, the U.S. Department of Agriculture in 1936 noted that there "is perhaps no darker chapter nor greater tragedy in the history of land occupancy and use in the United States than the story of the western range." Depletion of the range is "so nearly universal under all conditions of climate, topography, and ownership that the exceptions serve only to prove the rule." In the area studied, nearly all the western half of the country, virgin range had been depleted "no less than 52 percent," in the sense of reducing grazing capacity for domestic livestock.[12]

"In a nutshell, the white man's toll of the western range for 50 years . . . is reduced grazing capacity of more than half. Still further, 76 percent of the entire range has declined appreciably during the last 30 years and only 16 percent has improved," according to the report.[13]

This deterioration of the range was well known in government circles long before the 1930s. By 1923, Henry C. Wallace—secretary of agriculture and father of the future secretary of agriculture under President Franklin Roosevelt, Henry A. Wallace—was deploring the "reckless breakup of the range" by homesteaders. None of the public rangeland, except those acres that could be irrigated, was suitable for farming. Their "original forage producing value" was gone, at an "enormous loss" to the country, Wallace noted. He would establish range control through the U.S. Forest Service.[14] His successor, Secretary W. M. Jardine, in 1925 noted that homesteaders plowing up their land had "brought instability to the livestock industry, the open range continued to shrink in area and to deteriorate through overgrazing; erosion and floods followed."[15] By 1928 the U.S. General Land Office reported that all available public lands where dry farming of 640 acres would support a family had been taken up.

In 1929 President Herbert Hoover addressed this issue with an alternative to federal land ownership. He determined that western states were "more competent" to manage public lands, and he would convey 190 million acres of unappropriated land plus 45 million acres of withdrawn land (for stock driveways and coal and shale reserves) to the states for public school purposes.[16] This plan, however, did not include the conveyance of mineral rights, and most states were not interested.

As both the drought and depression worsened, Hoover called three hundred agricultural experts to a national conference on land utilization, at Chicago in November 1931. It was to recommend "a course of sanity" in those trying times.[17]

One government economist listed the agricultural maladjustments. The 1930 exchange value of farm products versus the cost of commodities the farmer must buy is "now 42 percent below pre-war levels and lower than at any time in more than a generation." Farm property taxes are two and a half times larger than in pre-war days, consuming more than eight percent of gross farm income. Farm mortgage debt is nearly three times that of twenty years ago, with an annual interest outlay of 560 million dollars. About one-third of the cultivated lands is "badly eroding" and up to twenty-five million acres "have been destroyed beyond recovery." Farm bankruptcies and foreclosures "continued at abnormally high levels" and in 1930 more than half of all farmers rented from other landowners. "At no time in our history has there been such a large proportion of the farmers renting the land they farm." Farm tax delinquency had rapidly mounted, as well.[18]

Elwood Mead, a great advocate of federal dam projects, presented the case for reclamation of arid lands through irrigation to the conference. No activity, he said, has "brought greater private and public benefits to the Nation than have come from the money spent on these Government reservoirs."

He warned that ending this activity would cause thousands of farms to be abandoned.[19] His plea went unheeded, as the conference recommended that only those reclamation projects currently underway be completed and no new ones be started.

The magic words for the conference instead became "land utilization" and "land use planning" as well as a firm belief that the federal government should be responsible for the remaining public lands. James C. Stone, chair of the Federal Farm Board, said it is hard to find "any part of our economic life in which there has been less careful planning than in the use of land. . . . A million or two of farm families are working pieces of land too poor to return a fair living." The primary objective of land utilization planning, he noted, is "to get families away from land that will not, however employed, yield as good a living as they can earn elsewhere; to get land laid out in tracts that can be operated more effectively . . . to shift land to other uses or combinations of uses promising more nearly adequate returns."[20] These were to become the watchwords for the incoming Roosevelt administration as well.

Conference recommendations included rehabilitating grazing lands with public administration, watershed protection, decentralizing population and industry, and reorganizing rural community land use to achieve local public economies.[21] There was also to be a national inventory of land resources. Marginal or submarginal land should be withdrawn from homestead entry and be added to the public range, a policy that was later enacted in part by passage of the 1934 Taylor Grazing Act. Even further, there should be federal land purchases for forest lands, wildlife refuges, parks and monuments, and soil conservation.[22]

Finally, the conference established a national land-use planning committee to promote its policies and recommendations, and this became the important Natural Resources Planning Board under President Roosevelt. New Dealers, in fact, were to embrace the heart of this conference as their own and adapt its policies to the social revolution they brought to America's lands.

2. Land, the First Essential

Euro-American settlement of the North American West was based on the goal of owning land, the most precious resource. The federal government was the settler's biggest partner in that objective. The government first appropriated the land, then explored it, wrenched it from its Native occupants, and protected it, dispersed it, and finally preserved what was left. Today twenty national grasslands are part of that heritage.

One of the strongest statements on the importance of land to humans was given by Nebraska historian Addison E. Sheldon in the introduction to his 1936 book, *Land Systems and Land Policies in Nebraska*. "Land is the first essential to the life of man on our planet," Sheldon wrote. Further, the regulatory system for using land "is the most important element in the success of any human society. . . . [N]o other one thing among the agreements under which men have inhabited this earth has been of so much importance as the conditions imposed by social consent, under which men might occupy and use the earth's surface."[1]

Lewis C. Gray, an important agricultural economist intimately involved in the New Deal bureaucracy, put it more bluntly. "The dominant characteristic of American economic life," he wrote, "has been abundance of land resources. The assumption of this abundance has colored our habits of thought and become the essential foundation for our economic policy, both individual and public."[2]

Precious as it is, however, American land historically has been mighty cheap, first given away freely in huge unexplored and unmapped chunks by royal patent and then taken through force of arms by the young nation and confirmed in the post–Revolutionary War peace treaty of 1783 between England and America. The 1803 Louisiana Purchase doubled the size of the nation for pennies an acre and added the lands that were to become the bulk of the national grasslands.

It became national policy, fed by the appetite of land speculators, to disperse this immense reserve quickly, and land sales were one of the country's early major sources of revenue. A complex structure of Indian treaties and land laws opened up America to settlement that worked well in the humid East and Middle West, but failed mightily in the semiarid Great Plains as farmers went bust trying to grow crops without enough water on too-small farms.

One government official tried to make sense of this frenzy to settle and farm arid lands under inappropriate humid land systems and habits. In 1879, John Wesley Powell presented one of the first land use plans designed to revolutionize land policy and farming methods in the West. A one-armed Civil War hero, Powell was head of the U.S. Geographical Survey, and his Report on the Lands of the Arid Region of the United States became one of the first national environmental studies.

Powell saw conditions for three types of land in the West: irrigable cropland, timber, and pasture. Irrigation, he thought, should be done cooperatively, with farmers combining labor and capital to construct canals or reservoirs, each family having small waterfront claims along streams, then fanning out to larger grassland and upland claims for livestock. Such land claims, Powell wrote, must be at least four square miles (2,560 acres) or even larger. This was far more than public law ever allowed. He predicted that if

3. Framed by Mount Shasta, Butte Valley National Grassland in northern California is an important stop on the migration route of many wetlands birds and hawks.

4. A Swainson's hawk fluffs its feathers, Butte Valley National Grassland.

5. The Little Missouri National Grassland of North Dakota is anything but little, comprising over one million acres of rolling hills and steep, river-eroded bluffs.

6. Blister beetles on purple locoweed in the Little Missouri National Grassland of North Dakota

land was surveyed in regular tracts on square-mile grids, "all the water sufficient for a number of pasturage farms may fall entirely within one division," leaving no water source for adjacent land.[3]

He was correct, of course, as ranchers throughout the American West
manipulated inadequate homestead laws to claim water rights and sources,
thus also controlling huge tracts of adjacent waterless land, worthless for
farming but excellent for grazing. Congress never approved Powell's ideas
and the familiar boom-and-bust of Western land settlement continued into
the twentieth century.

Another concerted look at rational land use policies occurred in the 1920s,
leading to the revolutionary reforms of the 1930s and the New Deal. The
twenties were memorable as the decade "in which the idea of limited agricultural growth first gained wide currency and seriously challenged the
traditional commitment to unlimited growth," according to one study. This
"rationalization of agriculture" not only meant "extensive land use changes" but also required "the retirement and reemployment of surplus farms
and surplus farmers," according to agricultural economist Albert Z. Guttenberg.[4] Specialized agricultural regions should be delineated with an eye
to "industrial efficiency, price maintenance, and conservation." The earlier
efforts by President Theodore Roosevelt to bring public interest to timber
lands through creating national forests "was now to be extended to crop and
pasture land," Guttenberg wrote.[5]

Lewis C. Gray, of the Bureau of Agricultural Economics in the U.S. Department of Agriculture, set the themes for land utilization policies for the
New Deal era with his seminal study in the 1923 USDA Agricultural Yearbook. Greater agricultural productivity would come from more intensive
farming practices, better crop selection, crop rotation, improved methods
of land preparation, and the use of higher-yield crop strains.[6] Gray and his
colleagues recommended a scientific land classification plan, programs to
protect wildlife in forests and marshes, recreational uses for wild lands, new
grazing districts on public rangeland using permits, and establishing a national agency to ensure the "recognition of the interrelatedness of all natural resource problems."[7] Land was classified as supermarginal, marginal,
and submarginal. Where submarginal land was found, "the people were to

be resettled on subsistence homesteads. Surplus land would be returned to timber and grass for recreation, wildlife reserves, and livestock pasture."[8]

Two recommended themes that were not recognized in the New Deal were Gray's suggestion that large-scale irrigation and drainage projects be dropped and that large crop subsidies were "profitless adventures."[9] As the Great Depression deepened, and the drought expanded and lengthened, relief efforts became very important. The Roosevelt administration initiated farm commodity subsidies that remain today and employed thousands of workers to build a great infrastructure of dams and reclamation projects throughout the West and elsewhere.

Along with land use policies and theories, the 1920s saw practical experiments in land utilization that, in miniature, forecast the national efforts of the New Deal. These occurred in Montana, South Dakota, and New York. M. L. Wilson, an agronomist who later became important in the New Deal Department of Agriculture, directed an "antecedent experiment" for the future Resettlement Administration and other government programs that eventually led to the national grasslands. One program, Fairway Farms in Montana, experimented in land use with resettlement and scientific farming.[10] In 1923, a group of agricultural economists conceived an idea of a company to rejuvenate farms and to help tenants become owners. With a $100,000 loan from John D. Rockefeller (at 5 percent interest but with no required repayment), Wilson incorporated Fairway Farms "to make experiments on the proper size of farms, the methods of selecting tenants and prospective owners, the most efficient equipping of farms, and the type of farming suited to a particular region." By 1926 he had purchased eight farm units of sizes varying up to 2,500 acres.[11]

All aspects of the experiment were to help tenant farmers "re-enter the national structure of freehold, one-family farms" and were "the first experiments in regional land use and were early precedents for the tenant-rehabilitation and [land] purchase programs of the New Deal."[12] The basic idea was to consolidate small submarginal tracts into family farms that could become supermarginal. While enjoying several successes, including complete mechanization and greater efficiency in production, "the drought and depression combined to make the Fairway Farms a financial failure. The project was discontinued and, much later, the land was sold."[13]

South Dakota initiated agricultural relief through programs of land acquisition in the 1920s. Governor Peter Norbeck acquired strategically located abandoned homesteads that had been used for dryland crop production and livestock grazing, and converted them back "to their original natural condition." He believed in government acquisition and ownership of the remaining vestiges of the wilderness frontier, according to one report, and some lands were later to become Custer State Park and part of the Badlands National Park in southwest South Dakota, adjacent to the present Buffalo Gap National Grassland.[14]

Perhaps most important for future New Deal programs was the work done in New York State by Governor Franklin D. Roosevelt, the future president. He had early on suggested "that suburban farms should be provided for city dwellers, thereby making city life tolerable." He supported an institutional link between city and country and advocated both suburban and rural planning. Under his governorship a temporary Emergency Relief Administration assisted many people back to the land.[15] He also sponsored experimentation and land surveys in Tompkins County, where submarginal land on hills near Cornell University "was removed from production and returned to grass and trees."[16]

The Tompkins County land survey was to be expanded statewide over ten years, with retirement and, usually, reforestation of submarginal land combined with a relief program for marginal farmers that included "tax adjustments, state aid for schools and roads, and rural electrification." Submarginal farmers would be resettled into what Roosevelt saw as a third type of American life (a marriage of agriculture and industry), which he named the "rural industrial group." This involved "industrial decentralization and a new balance between town and country." Rural life, Roosevelt believed, "had advantages which could not be duplicated in the city," and industry would "decentralize voluntarily."[17]

These views and experiments became substantial programs when President Roosevelt initiated the construction of one hundred communities in the early New Deal, first under the Division of Subsistence Homesteads in the Department of the Interior. They became a part of the social revolution of ending land dispersion under the Homestead Act, purchasing 11.3 million acres of submarginal land and establishing the eventual national grasslands.

After the national outcry for cheap or free land had died down, and rangeland observers became aware of abuses that had been piled on that land in the Great Plains and the West, there were calls for reform. New research, new economics, and new scientific knowledge led to new ideas of land use, especially of the millions of acres of public land. Papers were written, conferences were held, and experiments were tried; and then came drought and depression, transforming these ideas into real programs under the Roosevelt administration.

3. A Strange and Dramatic Moment

It was a strange and dramatic moment in American history. A failed president, by many measures a very good man, was overwhelmed by financial panic and the beginning of a decades-long drought. Farmers suffered from long years of economic depression even before the rest of the nation hit bottom, with big surpluses of grain and livestock, low commodity prices, high costs for equipment, supplies, and mortgages—and now no rain. Three years after the worst stock market collapse in history there were huge numbers of unemployed workers and shuttered factories across the land. There were very real fears of a revolution exploding, possibly with great violence, as family savings disappeared, cash became scarce, and people faced starvation and homelessness.

Then, on March 4, 1933, Franklin D. Roosevelt was inaugurated as president, replacing the beleaguered Herbert Hoover. Although he was at heart a fiscal conservative, even speaking about a balanced federal budget during his election campaign, Roosevelt and his advisors (including the famous

Brains Trust) knew they had to provide immediate relief for the panicked millions out of work and short of cash. Rexford G. Tugwell, an economist and member of Roosevelt's Brains Trust, wrote that Roosevelt "realized that several of his firmest notions, including pay-as-you-go and avoidance of doles, had been undermined by circumstances and had to be abandoned."[1] Roosevelt would attempt to buy his way out of the Depression, although that was never really possible until the end of the drought and mobilization for World War II began at the end of the decade.

Roosevelt's solution to the nation's ills, the New Deal, was a complex social, economic, and relief program. It offered reforms that were vilified by conservatives but were heralded by moderates and liberals as the true and necessary answer to problems. Throughout the many ins and outs of the New Deal, the U.S. Department of Agriculture proposed perhaps some of the most radical programs, along with widespread relief for the worst hit of the populace, America's farmers.

Henry A. Wallace was a highly appropriate choice for secretary of agriculture in this tumultuous time, serving from 1933 to 1940, after which he became a one-term vice president for Franklin Roosevelt. His father, Henry C. Wallace, had as secretary of agriculture in 1922 established the Bureau of Agricultural Economics (BAE), an important font of many of the ideas that later became active policy and new programs under the New Deal. The BAE reflected the elder Wallace's "interest in the economic side of agriculture and his conviction that the department should give as much attention to the market conditions that faced the farmer as it did to efforts to help him with production problems," according to one source. The younger Wallace mirrored that philosophy, seeking economists who viewed their profession as "something living, moving, active and directional in the world of affairs."[2] An idealist as well as a practical bureaucrat, Henry A. Wallace brought change to the department that plunged "it into the swift moving current of controversial economic and social reforms," according to the official history of the USDA.[3]

Rexford G. Tugwell became a major architect of that change. Born on a farm in western New York, he was educated and taught at eastern private universities and was an economics professor at Columbia University, New

York City, when he was recruited to the five-member Brains Trust of advisors for then Governor Roosevelt before his presidential campaign. Tugwell cut across the grain of traditional agrarian philosophy, which adored the Jeffersonian idea of the "superiority of agriculture as a way of life," rural values, individualism, independence, and free enterprise. However, the United States had become an industrial nation and Tugwell instead talked of absorbing "a very large number of persons from farms into our general industrial and urban life."[4] He was a self-proclaimed collectivist who felt that old institutions were obsolete in a world where science had "made possible a new world of plenty." New social institutions should be found "for the realization by all of the value of a surplus economy."[5] The Depression was caused by unequal income distribution, leading to less purchasing power by too many people, according to Tugwell. "There was too much scarcity in the midst of surpluses, all of which pointed to the necessity of institutional changes."[6]

After Roosevelt's inauguration, Tugwell joined the USDA as an assistant secretary and rather quickly rose to undersecretary. Seen as a misfit, "but a valuable misfit," Tugwell came from a liberal, urban university rather than the usual state agricultural college of most professors recruited to the USDA, whose "sympathies were most often with the larger farmers and the landowners." Tugwell instead looked to the downtrodden farm groups, tenants and farm workers, who "needed a labor union. Tugwell was more aware of rural poverty and degraded rural labor than most land-grant college graduates."[7] This fit well with FDR's ideas of social planning, sympathy for the poor, and back-to-the-land movements, although in the eventual political fallout over Tugwell and his perceived radicalism the ever-practical Roosevelt would allow the programs to adjust to the reality of special-interest politics.

At first, though, in the frenetic, famous, initial One Hundred Days of the Roosevelt administration, the ideals of the land utilization planners won out. They were joined with the "rural industrialist" idealists (including First Lady Eleanor Roosevelt) who pushed for new sustainable communities or subsistence homesteads for the urban unemployed as well as for poor farm families to be resettled from submarginal lands that would be purchased.

A presidential executive order created the National Resources Board that, in December 1934, recommended a long-term land acquisition policy to purchase seventy-five million acres and reclaim it to "demonstrate how it could be used to serve the public. It was recognized that it would, at the same time, be necessary to relocate the occupants or regroup them in suitable areas."[8]

Even before that report, however, the program moved forward. The biggest battle with Congress in the first months was to pass the Agricultural Adjustment Act (AAA). Its specific proposals concerned production controls with voluntary participation encouraged by rental or benefit payments, marketing and processing regulation and supervision, a processing tax to pay for the act, and an established parity price for commodities set at the 1909–14 base period.[9] By February 1934, the AAA administrators instituted a submarginal land purchase program, using $25 million provided through the Federal Emergency Relief Administration (FERA) Land Program, supplemented with work relief money to pay laborers for development work. This first land purchase was to buy about ten million acres in forty-five states, for the four stated uses of agricultural adjustments, Indian land, recreation, and wildlife refuges.[10] Lands purchased were commonly known as land utilization, or L-U, projects. By December 1934 there were sixty-four agricultural demonstration projects on nearly six million acres in forty-two states under active consideration for purchases at an average price of $5.25 per acre.

Details of the program included buying the same kind of lands as in the New York program developed by then Governor Roosevelt for withdrawing submarginal lands from cultivation. Thus, purchased land must be in cultivation but returning less income than expected for the work put into the farm, resulting in owners that "remain impoverished while working them." The land should also be suitable for development as forests, parks, recreation spaces, grazing ranges, bird or game refuges, or as additions to Indian reservations. Plantings and ground cover would protect against soil erosion. A definite plan of resettlement or reemployment would be worked out to ensure that people living on the land "may not become stranded or transient."[11]

The major weakness of this program, however, was in its administration.

Land purchase projects could be presented by any "interested department, bureau, or section" in the federal government. These would then be examined by the "several governmental departments concerned" to ensure full satisfaction. The land would then be turned "over to a Federal Department for its operation for the purpose of which it is best adapted." Technical direction of the land retirement funds and programs would be the dual responsibility of USDA and the Department of the Interior.[12]

L. C. Gray, who had moved over from the USDA's Bureau of Agricultural Economics to head the Land Policy Section of the AAA, saw the difficulty of reconciling special use policies with basic planning for submarginal land retirement. In the Great Plains, where the most lands were to be bought (and where they eventually became the majority of the national grasslands), Gray's purpose was to "see that semiarid land used for wheat or other arable farming was used for grazing instead." This meant that farms must become larger and low-income farm families must be resettled. In the nation's Northeast, land purchased would be converted to forests, game refuges, and recreational uses. In the South, where one-crop farming had depleted the land, projects would restore soil fertility and produce timber and wild game. Scattered and isolated farms in Great Lake states' forests put heavy burdens on local governments for services, so farmers there would be resettled in new model communities.[13]

The procedure for moving each land acquisition project ahead was also complex, according to a report by the secretary of agriculture. First, a "problem" area had to be identified where the conditions would demand readjustment, based on input from land use specialists, agricultural experiment station workers, state planning boards and conservation commissions, and other agencies. Before finding a project area, officials had to consider the economic status of the farmers; condition of the soil, native vegetation, and forests; and the need and purposes for public land. Further, relationships to nearby towns and cities, local opinion, and the attitudes of state agencies had to be gauged.

"Special consideration is given to the cost of the land and to the possibility of relieving unemployment by the development work on such a project," the report noted. Once projects were approved, boundaries were carefully defined and field men were told the probable value of the properties. Then they solicited proposals for sale by landowners, and the individual tracts were appraised before signing a formal sales offer. After tendering a sufficient number of formal offers, they submitted them to Washington for approval. Finally, the U.S. Department of Justice had to assure that land titles were sufficiently clear to transfer the land to the government in fee simple. This process, the report noted in unconscious irony, "has been found to require a considerable period of time." The government had never tried to buy so much land in so short a period, and the volume of work involved "has placed an unusual burden on the various administrative agencies affected," the secretary noted.[14]

A national survey found that about 454,000 farms on seventy-five million acres in the problem areas were on "land too poor to provide a living for their operators through crop farming." These lands, worth about $682 million in 1934, included twenty million acres of cropland, thirty-five million acres of pasture and range, and twenty million acres of forest. In 1929 the annual production of these farms equaled $204 million, but 45 percent of the crops and livestock grown was consumed on the farm, and only 55 percent was sold.[15]

In late 1934 and early 1935, the program envisioned purchasing 20,552,000 acres at an estimated cost of $104 million. Actual negotiations soon moved ahead to buy nine million acres on 206 of 250 proposed projects. However, administration of the projects was very loose. The Public Works Administration provided the funding, but selection, planning, and options for buying land was divided among the Land Policy Section of the Agricultural Adjustment Administration, the National Park Service, the Bureau of Biological Survey, and the Bureau of Indian Affairs. The Federal Emergency Relief Administration managed financial and legal matters, and its Division of Rural Rehabilitation resettled farm families. That division quickly fell behind in providing support and relief to farm families, which was further aggravated by the withdrawal of substantial drought relief funds slated for the program.[16]

Another beneficiary of the first Hundred Days of New Deal legislation was the subsistence homesteads program. After separate bills to establish the project failed to move ahead, sponsors included it as a section of the important National Industrial Recovery Act, enacted in May 1933. The section provided $25 million to aid the "redistribution of the overbalance of population in industrial centers," through loans or other aid to purchase subsistence homesteads, using any agencies the President may establish.[17]

As one analyst noted, "The subsistence homesteads program was left to be worked out by individuals within an action agency and without any clear mandate from Congress as to details. . . . This 'blank check,' so typical of the emergency legislation of 1933, would of necessity have to be written in terms of only a few of the many conflicting ideas about what subsistence homesteads should be. . . . The result was to be one of the most interesting social experiments in American history."[18]

President Roosevelt chose to place subsistence homesteads in the Department of the Interior, and Secretary Harold L. Ickes put M. L. Wilson (from the Montana Fairfield Farms experiment) in charge. Both the president and first lady took special interest in the project. Communities to be developed, near available employment, included four types: "experimental farm colonies, subsistence gardens for city workers, colonies for stranded workers, and, primarily, homesteads for part-time industrial workers."[19] In addition, Wilson "desired to establish a few all-rural colonies to absorb submarginal farmers and to demonstrate the possibilities of organized rural communities."[20] Loan requests of $4.5 billion were received, for the $25 million appropriated, indicating the huge emergency needs of the program.

Similar problems of administration complexity that the land purchase projects suffered hit the homesteads project, though they were not as overwhelming or extensive. Moreover, a major controversy arose as to house design and size for the communities, with some leaders wishing for small "shacks" while Mrs. Roosevelt and officials of the Division of Subsistence Homesteads "wanted bathrooms and plumbing in four- or five-room houses" to—as Wilson saw it—"demonstrate a new way of life."[21] The first lady won the debate, even over the president's wishes, but the controversy haunted the program throughout its life, raising severe criticism in the press and by conservative congress members over the perceived high costs and alleged luxurious construction.

All these problems, and more, festered on USDA undersecretary Tugwell, and after just one year into the New Deal he became discouraged. In addition to the land purchase and subsistence homesteads problems, rehabilitation work and erosion control on submarginal land by the Soil Erosion Service of the Department of the Interior lagged. There were problems of grazing controls on public lands, discovery of sharecroppers' ills through relief work, and continuing trouble in clearing land titles through the Justice Department.

In August 1934, Tugwell made a comprehensive report of the need to coordinate all these programs to the president and suggested "using an executive order to establish a coordinating agency operating with emergency funds."[22] The president agreed, and on May 1, 1935, he issued Executive Order 7027 creating the Resettlement Administration (RA), to be headed by Tugwell.

The president had earlier (November 1934) issued Executive Order 6910 that withdrew all remaining public lands, unreserved and unappropriated, in twelve Great Plains and West Coast states from settlement or sale. In addition, the Taylor Grazing Act of June 1934 authorized new grazing districts to include up to eighty million acres of public land under management of the Bureau of Land Management (but not the Forest Service), which were also withdrawn from homestead entry after public hearings. Under the act, the secretary of the interior was authorized to "initiate measures to protect, regulate the use of, and improve the lands within the districts."[23] In February 1935, public lands from twelve additional states were withdrawn, "which for the moment halted [homestead] entries except those where rights previously existed."[24] Thus, federal land giveaways ended and land purchases began.

This all set the stage for the massive reorganization of federal rural relief efforts during the depth of the drought and economic depression. The new Resettlement Administration had four main tasks: suburban resettlement, rural rehabilitation, land utilization, and rural resettlement. Tugwell, not surprisingly, was most interested in suburban resettlement, especially in creating new garden or greenbelt cities, as well as land utilization of submarginal lands. He was less interested in rural rehabilitation, even though he had seen to the transfer of the Soil Erosion Service from Interior to USDA and transformed it into the new Soil Conservation Service. Still he recognized that rehabilitation was vitally necessary in the current emergency. He also had less interest in the rural resettlement program, especially the subsistence homestead communities he inherited from Interior. Will W. Alexander, RA's deputy director, noted that Tugwell's central conviction was that "much of the farm problem grew out of a fundamental misuse of land," and his greatest interest "remained in reclassification and utilization of land."[25] But, according to one report, Roosevelt told Tugwell that "if he wanted a new agency to deal with rural problems, he had to take the whole package."[26]

As an independent agency created by presidential fiat, a nagging problem, the RA was not authorized by congressional statute until very late in its life. Initially given about $48 million in presidential discretionary funds along with $18 million in Work Relief money for development labor, all land purchases and land use planning was handled by one of the four RA units, the Land Utilization Division.

For the whole decade-long operation of the RA and its successor agencies, suburban resettlement and land utilization were minor aspects—"the former accounting for about $36 million in expenditures, the latter arranging for the retirement of about nine million of a proposed fifty million or one hundred million acres—and both were somewhat controversial." The RA's largest and least controversial activity addressed rural rehabilitation, disbursing about $778 million in loans and some $152 million in grants. Rural resettlement into subsistence communities or homesteads, at a relatively minor cost of about $72 million, evolved into "by far the most controversial" of the RA's programs.[27]

In addition to the four main RA program divisions of suburban resettlement, rural rehabilitation, land utilization, and rural resettlement, there were twelve coordinate divisions: business management, construction, finance, information, investigation, labor relations, management, personnel, planning, procedure, special plans, and special skills. The nation was divided into eleven administrative regions to deliver services. Tugwell inherited 4,200 employees from the transferred agencies but filled most of the top administrative posts with his own people. Employment quickly ballooned to thirteen thousand people, showing that the RA "definitely was not set up as a temporary agency."[28]

Moving quickly in some of the most desperate months of the drought and Depression in 1936, the RA's "most spectacular effort" became its extensive program of aid to drought-stricken farmers. Its rural rehabilitation division provided loans to farmers and tenants, for food, clothing, feed, seed, livestock, equipment, repairs, and land. There was an 86 percent repayment rate on the $778 million loaned, with average loans of $421 and supplemental loans of $202, to nearly a million families. The RA distributed another $152 million in cash grants, conducted a large and highly popular debt-adjustment program to ease heavy mortgage problems, and provided valuable technical assistance to 455,000 families.[29]

Tugwell later noted that two-thirds to three-quarters of the drought-stricken families received some kind of assistance. "No one in the short grass country was happy. The worst of the region's problems had not been solved. But there was a general gratefulness that in their extremity no money or effort had been spared to bring the affected families assistance. There had been a minimum of red tape. . . . Help had simply been brought and not too many questions asked."[30]

For the future national grasslands, the work of the RA's Land Utilization Division was most important. "The program of land use adjustment is the most extensive one yet undertaken by the Federal Government for the acquisition of lands now in private ownership," according to the agency's first annual report.[31] By the end of fiscal year 1936–37, 206 land purchase projects in forty-five states were approved, for a total of 9,149,000 acres. The majority of acres, 6,806,000, were for agricultural adjustment with the rest devoted to recreational, wildlife, and Indian projects.[32] Eventually a total of 11.3 million acres would be purchased, with almost 4 million acres becoming national grasslands.

When the RA was organized, Tugwell estimated there were 650,000 farm families on about 100 million acres of poor land, "which even experts could not have farmed at a profit." He did not plan to acquire all of this land and, in fact, recommended "adjustment" by restoring the land and good technical education to farmers over "simple retirement" as the best policy. However, retirement of land beyond hope of rehabilitation was appropriate in many cases, and the first step was to purchase, from voluntary sellers, the worn-out land. The land was then turned to non-farming uses—wildlife, recreation, Indian reserves, grazing, and forests.[33]

The Land Utilization Division had more than two hundred work projects to care for retired land and to carry out conservation work—in conjunction with the Soil Conservation Service—to control soil erosion, seacoast erosion, stream pollution, and flooding.[34] While some of the retired land had simply been abandoned or was held by outside interests without being worked by tenant farmers, much of the land was taken over from existing farm families who would have to leave their homes. Some departed to cities or other areas for other opportunities; those who did not were resettled on federal projects.

L. C. Gray noted that "[a] marginal land program without an associated program of resettlement would be largely futile; a program for establishing new communities or holdings unrelated to a land planning and land adjustment [rehabilitation] program would be meaningless."[35] Since proceeds from the land sale were often less than the family debt on the farm, relief loans and grants were needed. "Without help, it was likely they would purchase poor land, again drift into poverty, and repeat the cycle of ownership, debt, losses, failure, and public relief," one report noted.[36]

The RA's Rural Resettlement Division assumed control of the plans for all rural resettlement communities from the Division of Subsistence Homesteads in the Department of the Interior. These included thirty-four "industrial" and related projects with sixty-five communities across the nation, providing 3,304 housing units at an average cost of $9,114. Another twenty-eight communities were inherited from the Federal Emergency Relief Administration, including eight farm villages in Nebraska and one each in South Dakota and North Dakota. There were 2,426 housing units built at an average cost of $8,887. Indeed the RA's Rural Resettlement Division initiated more than 100 rural projects, including thirty-four communities, with 2,941 housing units costing an average of $6,878 per unit.[37]

The agency constantly struggled for funding to complete these and many other projects. The RA under Tugwell and the Works Progress Administration (WPA) under Harry Hopkins both received their money under the Emergency Relief Act of 1935, and the RA had to use relief labor under WPA regulations. "Thus, there was friction over labor and construction projects and jurisdiction of land-utilization projects, which used WPA labor, as well as continuous competition between Tugwell and Hopkins for executive funds," according to historian Bernard Sternsher. "This scrambling for dollars would not have occurred if the RA had attained legitimacy through the replacement of its enabling executive order by a legislative act."[38]

Congress enacted that enabling legislation only after Rexford Tugwell left the Resettlement Administration and government service in December 1936, after President Roosevelt won his second presidential election. The press and his enemies had nicknamed Tugwell "Rex the Red" and "Rex the Dreamer" for his controversial beliefs and program administration. "In terms of a contradictory image, Tugwell was both a dangerous threat to the American way of life and too ineffective to carry out his administrative duties," according to his biographer.[39] One critic noted that "Tugwell knew little about agriculture but a great deal about crusades." Very quickly, attacks on Tugwell became "inseparable from criticism of the agency which he headed."[40]

President Roosevelt passed on to Tugwell unfavorable comments on the RA received at the White House and complained in August 1936 about the high unit cost of some resettlement projects, saying "I do not think we have a leg to stand on."[41]

Among the harshest of congressional critics was Senator W. Warren Barbour of New Jersey, who in March 1936 sought an investigation of the RA's spending, nature and extent of current and future projects, effect of projects on local taxes and real estate values, selection of tenants, and more. Barbour emphasized the "enormous size" of the RA, with sixteen divisions located in twenty-seven buildings, its own telephone exchange, and a large number of workers. Instead of the investigation, the senator settled for a full report of its work, which Tugwell submitted on May 12, 1936.[42]

To sum up, the RA faced imposing obstacles: extremely difficult goals, federal agency competition, a hostile press, poor clients, and a majority population that held minimal concern for the problems of rural people.[43]

7. Remnants of tallgrass prairie exist among the
wooded fields of the Sheyenne River National
Grassland.

8. Cedar River National Grassland, North Dakota

9. Grand River National Grassland in South Dakota provides habitat and hunting opportunities for deer, pronghorn, pheasant, and waterfowl.

10. With miles and miles of unobstructed views and endless grass prairies, South Dakota's Fort Pierre National Grassland captures the essence of the national grasslands.

11. Abandoned farmstead, Buffalo Gap National Grassland.

12. Toadstool Geologic Park lies within the Oglala National Grassland of northwest Nebraska.

13. A passing storm crosses the varied
terrain of the Oglala National Grassland.

14. Sunset over the high plains of the Oglala
National Grassland of northwest Nebraska

On Tugwell's last day of service, December 31, 1936, a presidential executive order transferred the RA to the Department of Agriculture, ending its nearly two-year history as an independent agency. The Bankhead-Jones Farm Tenant Act was passed in July 1937, finally giving congressional authorization to the RA, which in September was renamed the Farm Security Administration. The law also limited the controversial resettlement community and land utilization programs to finish only projects under way.

Title III of the Bankhead-Jones Act, Retirement of Submarginal Land, finally gave congressional approval to correct maladjustments in land use and purchases of submarginal lands. The law is unique, as "it expressly requires that the land be managed for conservation and wildlife. The Act is silent as to whether grazing is even a permitted activity on the land," according to one report.[44]

In a game of musical chairs, federal control of the L-U projects went to the Soil Conservation Service on October 16, 1938, and land purchases were continued until February 1943, when that program ended except for minor acquisitions or land trades.[45] The SCS continued rehabilitation of the 11.3 million acres purchased including reseeding, grazing management, and small dam construction, until the lands were transferred to the U.S. Forest Service of the USDA on November 2, 1953. The new mandate ensured a "sustained yield" of the grasses as well as multiple use of the land under the Forest Service.[46]

Land utilization projects were all reviewed, in 1954, to find their best use. Eventually states and nonfederal agencies received certain lands most suitably determined for specialized uses. Thirteen forest areas became national forests. The Bureau of Land Management received lands in Montana, California, New Mexico, Texas, and Utah, as part of grazing districts administered by the BLM, with many of the transfers vigorously protested by the U.S. Forest Service. The Montana congressional delegation was at odds with the Forest Service and demanded that their huge state L-U projects go to the BLM. On June 20, 1960, the remaining 3,804,000 acres were designated as nineteen national grasslands under the Forest Service, to be managed for outdoor recreation, range, timber, watersheds, and wildlife and fish management purposes. The twentieth grassland of 18,425 acres, Butte Valley National Grassland in northern California, was dedicated in July 1991, as part of the Klamath National Forest.

In the history of the L-U projects' land purchases leading up to the national grasslands and other uses, a total of 11,299,000 acres were bought between 1933 and 1946, including more than thirty-seven thousand individual units. The total cost was $47.5 million (or about $4.50 per acre), exclusive of public domain lands already owned by the federal government and the cost of appraising, negotiating, and title clearance. All land improvements and development through 1954 cost the government $102.5 million, bringing the total cost of the L-U projects to $150 million, or about $13.50 per acre.

Development work included general land treatment, infrastructure and transportation improvements, control of erosion, flood control, water storage, and development for forestry, recreation, and wildlife. "Buildings and fences were removed; old roads no longer needed were blocked up; new roads were built where needed; suitable areas were seeded to grass or planted in trees; forest stands were improved and protected from fire; gullies were stopped; terraces, stock ponds, and dams were built; and stream channels were widened and cleaned." This was nearly all accomplished by local workers, a large number furnished by the Works Progress Administration. Relief jobs were provided in the first few weeks for fifty thousand or more workers, and for thirteen thousand men whose farms had been purchased, according to one L-U projects history.[47]

4. Broken-up Badlands, Thin Threads of Trees

One of the original nineteen grasslands, Oglala NG consists today of 94,435 acres in Nebraska. It is in northern Sioux and Dawes Counties, on the South Dakota border, adjoining Buffalo Gap NG in that state. Located on gumbo land, much of the Oglala NG is Pierre shale or clay. It also contains broken-up badlands, with thin threads of trees only along the riverbanks and edging down from the Pine Ridge's high buttes to the south. There are also alkaline flats, dried up with little life existing on them. Although the land was not as badly misused as that in the 1930s' Dust Bowl of the Southern Great Plains, there were many abandoned farms at the time of the land purchases.

Drought conditions throughout the 1920s and 1930s culminated in the driest year, 1934. All farm commodity prices were at record lows. Corn, which sold for $1.56 per bushel in 1920, had dropped to thirteen cents per bushel in 1932. Wheat went from $2.08 to twenty-seven cents per bushel. Oats were selling for a dime a bushel and barley for thirteen cents. In 1929

cattle were at a high price of $11.06 per hundredweight and three years lat-
er were selling for $4.10. Grass on the range died out, and there was vir-
tually no pasture for livestock. Cattle were starving and the government
purchased (and destroyed) livestock nationwide, just to give farmers and
ranchers some cash for relief.[1]

In the midst of this devastation, the opportunity to sell out and relocate
on more productive land with a new house or to just have some cash for vital necessities or to move on, must have seemed like a gift from heaven. As
early as 1933, the Farm Credit Administration formed a committee of volunteers in Sioux County to bring debtors and creditors together to reach a
"satisfactory adjustment of mortgages and other debts." This process was
taken over by the Resettlement Administration in 1935, which could then advance money to farm families to purchase or lease land in a loan program.
Those eligible were farmers on marginal land, "which will not yield a satisfactory living," tenants, and young married couples just starting out.[2] In November 1935, the state of Nebraska announced a debt conciliation program
to assist in settling cases, without court action, where debt was clearly more
than could be paid and foreclosure was eminent. Local committees would
"devise an adjustment" agreeable to both parties.[3]

However, in many cases the solution to overwhelming debt and poverty
was to sell out to the federal government, which at the time was about the
only entity buying land. Under the old AAA programs, federal appraisers
were sent to the field as early as 1933 to help set up land purchases. This ac-
celerated with the birth of the Resettlement Administration. Sioux County's
only newspaper, the weekly Harrison Sun, announced in late 1935 that about
$700,000 was available to purchase some 155,000 acres in Sioux and Dawes
Counties.

The purchases would be of "dry land farms, drought damaged ranges, abandoned crop land, cut-over woodlands and young timber on the Pine Ridge
Escarpment." Those areas would then be developed for grazing, forestry, and
recreation, along with flood control, water conservation, game preservation,
and an addition to a state park.[4] The aim was to shift land unsuited for cropping over to grazing use. "The development of large, well-managed grazing
areas should enable the farmers and ranchers to obtain a more stable income

than is possible under present conditions and the grass cover will protect the soil from further erosion," according to a 1937 RA press release in Nebraska.[5] E. P. Wilson, an historian writing in 1938, noted that the "ultimate readjustment" of use for the federal purchases of Nebraska Panhandle "high risk land" was to "return thousands of acres of land turned wrong side up by plows during the World War [I] period to grass and tree growth," and to prevent such actions in the future. The aim was to assure long-term tenure to ranch families within the area.[6]

For those selling out and leaving, resettlement was available at eight RA farmstead project sites in Nebraska. These were located at Scottsbluff, Loup City, Kearney, Grand Island, Fairbury, Falls City, South Sioux City, and at Two Rivers, twenty miles north of Omaha. As late as September 1938 there were still vacancies on these projects. There, successful applicants would live in a "new, modern home" where they could "raise a garden, chickens, have a cow and a sow," and join a cooperative farming enterprise with financial and technical help from the Farm Security Administration. Leases were available for "very reasonable terms" with the chance to buy the farmsteads later.[7] Some of the homes are still standing west of Scottsbluff.

But in reality, 41 percent of the L-U land purchases were from absentee individuals, families, or institutions outside the Sioux County area, often from other states.[8] An examination, case by case, of 319 tracts purchased (involving the vast majority of land in the Oglala NG) shows 189 tracts purchased from people in Sioux or Dawes Counties, or contiguous counties in South Dakota or Wyoming. Purchases outside that three-state area totaled 129 tracts. Four cases were uncertain, according to the reports. Some of those out-of-area purchases were from former residents who had already moved elsewhere. In several cases, Jane and John Doe were listed as owners, as the records were unclear as to who the owners were or where they lived. This was also often the case in estate settlements, when the exact list of heirs was unknown. Public and private institutions were involved in at least twenty-two tracts, including out-of-area corporations, federal courts, Sioux or Dawes County delinquent tax lands, and banks. In two cases, land mortgaged by failed banks was sold to repay depositors who had claims on the banks.

Of the 319 tracts, records show that 139 were leased at the time of appraisal. Some sort of improvements, beyond fencing, existed on 112 tracts. This could include an elaborate ranch headquarters with house and outbuildings. Usually, however, the improvements were listed as old homes, wells and windmills, sheds and outbuildings, and dams. Most tracts had no improvements.

Until the appraisal forms changed in the later years of L-U purchases, there was a place for field men to list why the land should be purchased, and those comments are revealing about the nature of the national grassland program. In sixteen cases, "owner wishes to sell" was given as the reason for purchase. In twenty-one cases, the purchase was to fill in a block of land. "Overgrazed" was the comment on fourteen tracts, and "submarginal" land was noted twice. Nonresident status of ownership was given nineteen times. Good timberland was noted on forty-two tracts. Good grazing ground was noted on thirty-six tracts and "for development" on twenty-two tracts.

One of the most frequent comments, on forty tracts, was the equivalent of "no income to owner," with "heavy debt" listed on four tracts. For thirty-five tracts, the comment was "not large enough unit" or not a "suitable" farm. Condemnations accounted for nine tracts. In at least one case, the appraiser recommended that land not be purchased, writing, "These people are thrifty and can make a living on this tract." However, the land, 760 acres plus improvements, was purchased for $2,827.20. Prices for land ranged from fifty cents per acre for "waste," up to $4 and $4.50 for good farmland, including the more tillable loam soils. Most land sold for two and three dollars per acre.

Among the tracts sold was one by William M. Forbes, a single man, on September 10, 1936. He had two hundred acres in Dawes County, which sold for an average of a dollar per acre. Forty acres sold for $2 each, another forty were listed at $1.50 each, and 120 acres of wasteland sold for fifty cents an acre. Notes by the appraiser indicate the owner leased out the land, apparently for grazing, and there were no improvements shown or paid for. The owner had the right to occupy and graze the land under a temporary cropping agreement, to February 28, 1937. Forbes received his two hundred dollars in cash on October 21, 1936.

On another tract, Benjamin F. Pitman, a widower, sold 2,400 acres in

Dawes County for prices ranging from $1.60 to $4.50 per acre. There was "good buffalo and wheat grass on 1,855 acres," according to the appraiser, with a lower grade on 120 acres of farmland and 25 acres of wasteland (sold for fifty cents an acre). This was a substantial holding, with a five-year-old frame house, barn, granary, corral, three wells, 1,600 rods of fencing, and two dams. The improvements brought an additional $2,340 for Pitman and his total sale was $9,491.50 on April 23, 1937, a small fortune at the time.

A survivor of the Great Depression was Albert Meng, who with his wife, Helen, as newlyweds in 1934 lived through the heart of the Dirty Thirties in Sioux County. Helen Meng died on November 27, 1994; Albert Meng died on September 7, 1998. The couple sold three tracts of land to the federal government under the resettlement program, although they remained as ranchers in the county. One tract of nearly 80 acres was sold for $168.22, and another 320 acres went for $1,019. They also sold nearly 375 acres near the now ghost town of Orella, Nebraska.[9]

Albert Meng recalled the times in a March 1994 interview. Life "got desperate" in the 1930s, and people were destitute and hungry. He said 1934 was a bad year, the worst one ever to hit the county. It was dry, with a total rainfall of 4.5 inches that entire year, he remembered. Cattle were sold out of the county when possible. But Meng witnessed the government buying up cattle and watched as ditches were dug and diseased and emaciated cattle shot there and buried. Calves sold for six dollars per head, tops, and sixteen to eighteen dollars for cows, Meng said. Cattle in good shape were butchered for their meat, which was given out as relief supplies.

Meng recalled he got a government loan and bought thirty head of cattle at thirty dollars a head to feed over the winter. He bought cane, a form of Sudan grass, for thirty dollars a ton at nearby Whitney, Nebraska, with a one-ton bundle needed for each cow. However, in early May there was a snowstorm. "We lost a bunch of calves," he said. "But we survived." As an indication of how tough times were, Meng said his father was treasurer of the local phone line, and a neighbor came in to pay his annual bill of three dollars. "He counted out the change and had a little left, and would have no more money for a year," Meng said. "He didn't know where any more money would come from."

When land in Sioux County was sold to the government, Albert Meng described how field men would appraise the tract and make a bid. "Misrepresentation was done at times, because the appraisers got a bonus for each lot sold," he said. Appraisers told people they could sell their ranch headquarters and lease it back, but they were then forced to move off, Meng claimed. This practice was also noted by another survivor of the times, Carroll Schnurr, a former legal secretary in Harrison. She grew up in the area when land "was acquired by the government through misrepresentation, condemnation, or otherwise," she wrote in a letter. Federal agents contacted her parents about selling their ranch and told them they could sell to the government and live on the place "at less cost than owning it." This seemed too good to be true, so her parents decided not to sell. "People who were influenced by the government agents were less fortunate. After selling, they were forced to vacate the land. The improvements were demolished and burned. Some buildings were sold by sealed bids. My father acquired a few buildings for a very minimal amount, which he moved to his ranch," she wrote. A neighbor had his land condemned and was forced to sell for $3.50 an acre, she noted.[10]

In October 1938, the national submarginal land utilization program, encompassing 105 projects (including the Pine Ridge L-U project in Sioux and Dawes Counties) on 7.1 million acres was transferred to the Soil Conservation Service of the USDA. Land purchases continued chiefly in the Northern Great Plains, including some in Nebraska, with the emphasis on "acquiring larger areas and enlarging established agricultural adjustment projects." By 1943 all acquisitions ended with 11.3 million acres purchased nationally.[11] A brief report in the Harrison Sun noted that, in April 1939, the land buying program was being used "to set up more economical sized units in the Pine Ridge region."[12] There was much less need for relief and resettlement by then, so purchases were used mainly to fill in blocks. Even so, public and private lands are interspersed checkerboard style in the Oglala NG today.

As part of the management and rehabilitation of government lands purchased under the L-U program, the Sugarloaf Soil Conservation District was formed for Sioux and Dawes Counties. It served in lieu of establishing grazing districts, which are used to manage and lease much of the public range elsewhere in the West. Property owners within the district boundary created the soil conservation district by approving a referendum held on July 31, 1942. The district included 90,450 acres of federally owned land (the Oglala NG at that time), 12,475 acres of Nebraska state land, and 122,320 acres of private land, for a total of 225,335 acres.[13] The district rented the federal grasslands and then provided lease permits on small tracts back to area ranchers.

In 1970, the Sugarloaf Grazing Association incorporated the duties of the SCS district. A management plan was prepared and approved by the Forest Service, authorizing the association to pay a federally established grazing fee for most of the Oglala NG. The association then rents grazing privileges to member ranchers. A plan was approved for "the promotion of grassland agriculture, and sustain yield management of forage, fish and wildlife, water, recreation and minerals will be emphasized." Specific goals are outlined for livestock grazing, wildlife habitat, and riparian area management.[14]

Butch Ellis, a former Forest Service official in charge of grazing districts at the Forest Service headquarters in Chadron, explained the financial agreement in 1998 with the Sugarloaf Grazing Association. There are about 28,000 animal units per month (AUM) on the 94,000 grassland acres under grazing permits, for an average of 3.5 acres per AUM. One AUM is listed as a one-thousand-pound unit of livestock—cattle, sheep, or horse. For the Forest Service, a horse counts as 1.2 AUM, for example. Permits can run from May 1 through December annually, although most end on October 31. The cost to the Sugarloaf Association for an AUM was $1.35 in 1998, down from an earlier fee of $2.08 per AUM in 1994. It is $1.43 in 2004. "We sell the right to occupy the land [and] space for a certain number of livestock," Ellis said. The association then distributes permits to its members, usually a rancher with land contiguous to the grassland.[15]

Past president of the Sugarloaf Association, and son-in-law of the late Albert Meng, Wes Pettipiece, and his wife, Gerry, live on the Meng home ranch, isolated at the end of Sand Creek Road, north of Harrison. He said the association charged its members $6.50 per AUM for permits in 1994 and down to $4.25 in 1998, using the difference from the Forest Service fees as extra funds for maintenance and to hire a range rider to take head counts of livestock and check pastures. Nearly all improvements on federal land are cost-shared between the permit holders and the Forest Service, but belong to the federal government. Half of the AUM fee paid to the Forest Service goes to the U.S. Treasury and a fourth is used for conservation practice activities, such as spraying for noxious weeds, maintaining stock dams, and reseeding. The other 25 percent is used to pay in-lieu property taxes to Sioux County. In addition, some conservation dollars are used in pipeline construction to bring water for livestock and homesteads from wells on and near the Pine Ridge. Water is delivered to stock tanks in the pastures and to ranch houses.[16]

The Oglala NG and its history is an almost perfect example of how the grasslands came to be. In desperate times of drought and economic depression, the federal government came up with cash to buy depleted land from starving farmers and ranchers, built them a house on a small plot, and hired hundreds of them to rehabilitate the land. The land stayed in the public realm and a unique partnership between ranchers and the Forest Service allowed private cattle grazing on the land. Despite some abuses by government buyers, the whole plan worked. Out of it has come a large block of grassland, open to the public and managed for wildlife and recreation, as well as private grazing.

5. Highest Purpose of the Grasslands

About ten thousand years ago the Wisconsin, the last glacier on the Great Plains, died and retreated northward. Along with the drying and warming effect of the rain shadow formed by the Rocky Mountains to the west, that glacial retreat (a time period of 90 to 174 years) drew the covering boreal spruce-pine forest with it, to be replaced briefly (for about 200 years) with oak woodland, in the Great Plains. The conversion to grasslands took about another 150 years, "making the total time for transition from a glacier-dominated boreal forest to a relatively arid grassland less than 600 years," according to one authority. The conversion from forests to grassland served as a "magnet, attracting plants, especially grasses, that were adapted to take advantage of the newly created condition."[1] Thus the grasslands, as known then by the Native American inhabitants of the Great Plains and later by the first European explorers and settlers, are very young in geological time. Most of the species flowed in from other areas, with "few natives among its flora and fauna."[2]

The grassland biome in the vast heartland plains of America constitut-
ed one of the largest ecosystems in the world, before Euro-American settlement, and still represents one of the greatest natural assets of the Great
Plains. Most native tallgrass prairies of the eastern, wetter fringe of the Great
Plains have disappeared, replaced by grain cultivation, urban development,
public facilities and infrastructure, and pastures often planted in lush im-
ported grasses. But in the semiarid lands generally west of the hundredth
meridian, native mixed and shortgrass prairies still survive and support es-
sentially the same use as pre-European settlement: grazing by large mammals, cattle now instead of bison. In fact, anthropologist Douglas Bamforth
notes that grazing pressure "exerted by bison and other herbivores on the
Great Plains before the mid-1880s was probably more or less constant as a
result of a long period of mutual adaptation of grasses, herbivores, and the
herbivores' predators (including human beings)." Bamforth also noted that
although the mixed prairie domination was first explained as the result of
historic overgrazing, it is now recognized as a "natural condition and di-
vides the High Plains into an eastern mixed prairie section and a western
shortgrass prairie section," extending from the hundredth meridian west to
the Rockies and from Saskatchewan to central Texas.[3]

Although the switch from a boreal forest environment took less than a
blink of an eye in geological time, it still involved about six centuries. Studies of the devastating drought of the 1930s showed that, in contrast, along
with the intervention of humans, long-term (even permanent) changes in
the grasslands could take place in a decade or even mere years. That conclu-
sion was a surprise to many believers in the climatic climax theory of grassland species succession. One was John E. Weaver, a biologist who studied
the drought in great detail and who had led research at the University of Nebraska prior to the Dust Bowl. He argued that "grasslands plants behaved as
a community, not as individuals, and that the entire mid-continental grassland represented one vast formation." The contemporary shortgrass prairie
found before the drought resulted only from overgrazing of the mixed-grass
prairie, the true or climax prairie that would dominate except for human
intervention, he believed. Weaver "could not conceive of circumstances under which the plants might naturally be destroyed, or under which mainte-

nance of the plains structure would require human intervention."[4]

That belief was overturned by the end of the 1930s drought. Weaver admitted that "man could permanently alter the structure of the grasslands." Vegetational succession was progressive, but only if independent of human interference. If that interference was permanent, then "only man could put the succession back in the direction of climatic development. Man so inextricably wove himself into the ecological fabric of nature that he could not be neutral; either he destroyed or he promoted. 'Nature' could not guide vegetation toward the climatic climax, or repair damage, because nature, as action of a natural world independent of man, simply did not exist—certainly not in the mid-continental grasslands." To actively guide grasslands to succession, then, was called conservation, and required human intervention.[5]

Conservation is the current stage of development of the national grasslands, after the traumatic adventures of drought, land purchases, and bureaucratic high jinks were played out. By the end of 1940, according to one history, "most of the initial acquisition and development work had been completed on all [L-U] projects started before passage of the Bankhead-Jones Farm Tenant Act." The projects had been transferred to the Soil Conservation Service in 1938, but the big job of rehabilitation waited until 1946, after World War II. From 1946 to 1954 (when the U.S. Forest Service took over) many bare and idle submarginal lands were planted in grass and trees and were managed by local grazing associations or soil conservation districts. They emphasized large-scale structural developments, including "stock water ponds, reservoirs, erosion control works, fire towers, construction of fire control lands and access roads, planting trees, and seeding grasslands to improve plant species—especially crested wheatgrass," according to one authority.[6]

By 1960, the L-U projects were divided out and twenty-two of them in eleven states became the initial twenty national grasslands, seventeen located in the Great Plains plus one each in Idaho and Oregon. The Butte Valley L-U project in California was accepted as a national grassland in July 1991. In 1960, 71 percent of the grasslands acres were managed under cooperative agreements with grazing associations and 29 percent under direct permits and leases. The highest purpose of the grasslands is "to serve as demonstration areas to show how lands classified as unsuitable for cultivation may be converted to grass for the benefit of both land and people in the areas. Under careful management, they are being developed for greater sustained yields of grass, water, wildlife, and trees; they also offer opportunities for outdoor recreation," according to an official history.[7]

In the beginning of the soil rehabilitation effort, not much was known about restoring wind-eroded lands back to grass. Estimates of restoration ranged from twenty-five to forty years, depending on various factors, but experts wanted a speedier result, so a technical program to stabilize blowing lands began, especially in the Dust Bowl areas, according to one history of the times. The first process was to mechanically list the "blow lands" so deep furrows caught soil and held moisture. Then drought-resistant cover crops were planted, such as black amber cane and Sudan grass, "to reduce wind velocity at ground level and thereby hold moving soil." Listing and plantings were often done two or three times before wind erosion stopped, and the scs specialists hoped that even weeds would cover the land, rather than see the bare soil. "In the absence of the best grasses, the scs utilized weeds, such as the Russian thistle, to hold the soil rather than to let it remain barren and exposed to the wind."[8]

In one experiment in eastern Montana non-native crested wheatgrass was used to reseed ten-acre plots on twenty-five farms and ranches. They found that deeper, four-inch furrows with five-pound-per-acre seeding worked best and "came through the 1931 and 1934 droughts without loss of stand," according to historian William D. Rowley. Later the scs "successfully seeded millions of depleted range acres in the Great Plains from North Dakota to southern Colorado, using these research results."[9] Although it is a quick-growing bunch grass that does well on eroded ground, crested wheatgrass is most nutritious in spring months and drops out as a good forage crop in summer and fall months.[10] While still present on many national grasslands, crested wheatgrass is a poor competitor against other grasses such as blue grama, buffalo grass, sideoats grama, western wheatgrass, and big and little bluestem.

By the mid-1930s, Rowley noted, Forest Service supervisors described their management philosophy as "multiple use," as they attempted to adjust to new demands on public lands. This became more pronounced in later years and is most important today. The decade also saw a large increase in wildlife on L-U project acres, including a 140 percent increase in big game herds, as the Depression "reduced recreational hunting, permitting game populations to explode," Rowley wrote.[11]

A potential problem of wartime overgrazing was avoided during World War II as the Forest Service "held the line" on "extravagant requests" for increased livestock allotments from either producers or the Department of War Production. "Forest grazing officials effectively used the argument that a sudden increase in livestock would not increase production, but only damage the ranges to the point that they would be completely unproductive," Rowley wrote.[12] In fact postwar plans for the Forest Service called for livestock reductions on public ranges in all states, noting that rancher incomes would not be affected because "larger animals kept the general income up."[13]

Stockmen's dissatisfaction with the Forest Service over livestock reductions, fees, the right to transfer use of grazing permits, and other issues led to congressional attention following the war. Congressman Frank A. Barrett of Wyoming opened House committee hearings on the Service, including public meetings throughout the West, with an aim toward transferring L-U projects and other public lands back to the states or into private hands. This created a public outcry against a "land grab" with Bernard DeVoto, editor and noted writer for Harper's magazine, being the most influential voice. DeVoto said the ultimate objective was private ownership of "all public lands in the western states, which would mean the end of conservation and watershed protection."[14] Representative Barrett and other critics hoped for a postwar reaction against "New Dealism" and the agencies that ruled the public lands and resources. However, as Rowley noted, "the Forest Service had a longer history than the New Deal, and its roots of support went deeper into the soil of American reform than the crisis of the recent depression."[15]

Still, the Forest Service was not hidebound. When it acquired L-U project lands from the Soil Conservation Service, a sister USDA agency, "it also accepted their [SCS] patterns of grazing administration. It chose not to disturb long-established practices and demonstrated a flexibility rare in bureaucratic agencies." The SCS had a long-term policy of involving the lands of private users in shaping the use and grazing practices on adjoining public lands, and this continued by Forest Service cooperation with grazing districts on the larger L-U projects, especially in the Northern Great Plains.[16] It made great common sense, as well, because of the checkerboard look of the public lands, where land purchases were interspersed with private acres, as well as with public lands under control of various state (school lands and parks) and federal agencies including the Bureau of Land Management.

By the 1960s, Congress became more involved with the administration of L-U projects and other public lands, beginning by passing the Multiple Use–Sustained Yield Act of 1960 supporting conservationism. The decade witnessed greater multiple uses, while achieving proper economic and environmental efficiency. The 1960 law directly stated that, for the first time, national forests (but not including national grasslands) "shall be administered for outdoor recreation, range, timber, watershed, and wildlife and fish purposes."[17] For Forest Service rangers on grasslands this became a USDA administrative order where range improvements involved proper cattle stocking, applying a sound grazing plan, removing harmful or useless vegetation, reseeding efforts, and coordinating livestock use with other forest uses such as wildlife, watersheds, and timber production.[18]

By the end of the 1960s, a new environmental movement spread across the nation, and this led to the 1969 National Environmental Protection Act. Its effect on Forest Service lands required environmental impact statements for all management plans and "public hearings focused on grazing as an environmental question as well as a management process." Attention focused on wildlife habitat and native plant values as well as objections to uses of herbicides and other chemicals in reseeding management. A 1972 Forest Service study, The Nation's Range Resources, declared much of the western range, both public and private, to be "in a deteriorating condition." While there was a need for as much as $183 million for range management, the Forest Service and Bureau of Land Management together were able to spend only about $27 million.[19]

15. Passing coal trains, Thunder Basin National Grassland

16. The Pawnee Buttes geologic formation rises 350 feet over the plains on the Pawnee National Grassland of northeast Colorado.

17. Cow and passing spring storm on a national grassland pasture, Pawnee National Grassland

This led to further congressional action with the Federal Land Policy and Management Act of 1976. This law provided funding for environmental impact statements on livestock grazing in the eleven western states, a range-betterment fund, and "more secure tenure for livestock grazing," but it was expressly limited to national forests, not grasslands. Importantly, it also ended the "land grab" debate by acknowledging that Congress intended the federal government to "retain perpetually the public lands in its ownership." A follow-up law was the Public Rangelands Improvement Act of 1978, which launched a "stewardship program" where ranchers received greatly reduced grazing fees for their cooperation in large pilot projects of combined management with the Forest Service and BLM, but again exempting the national grasslands.[20]

The Wilderness Act of 1964, while particularly important in mountain and alpine areas, has had some peripheral impact on national grasslands. The law protects a variety of ecosystems through establishing wilderness areas, and this has been contemplated in some long-term planning on the grasslands.

Even more important is the 1973 Endangered Species Act, where "management can change drastically if a threatened or endangered species has a primary habitat on the grasslands. If the species is found to be endangered, all development could be halted and grazing may be restricted," according to Leslie Aileen Duram. Several grasslands have been and may be affected by this law.[21]

But management of the national grasslands is more than congressional acts and policies from Washington. On the ground, it all depends on people working with the land and those who use it for all sorts of purposes. Terry West, a Forest Service historian, saw that ever since its birth in 1905, the Forest Service mainly employed foresters working on the national forests. Suddenly, in 1953, "it found itself charged with care of a new type of resource—treeless, flat, grasslands. Those early employees who were assigned to work on the grasslands sometimes felt forgotten by the rest of the agency."

One ranger expounded, "A lot of people (in the Forest Service) felt that when you were sent to the national grasslands that it was like being shipped to Siberia in the agency. But, for many, once they were there a few years, they never wanted to return to the national forests."

West noted that there was a trend toward segregation of the two staffs and this placed grasslands people "at a disadvantage" in job advancement. One grasslands employee interviewed in the 1970s said: "I think the Forest Service thought the grasslands was a desert, and they still do not think much different: they kind of look down on the grasslands—there are no trees."

On the other hand, grassland employees had a great deal of independence because of reduced supervision and decentralized management. West quotes Deen Boe, on the grassland from 1967 to 1972, who felt misunderstood or ignored by Forest Service officials, but then "we ran the national grasslands on our own." Rangers had great leeway, he said, with few rules to bind them. And grazing associations in the northern plains dealt with the daily operations. "The Bankhead-Jones Act was not very specific on L-U lands."

Because the grasslands are mostly dispersed units intermingled with state, private, and other federal lands, there must be "integrated resource management" as projects on one parcel of land affect neighboring lands. Thus rangers must do active outreach work, West said. This difference in outlook from forest work was so important to one ranger that he thought all rangers should work on national grasslands to get a broader resource management picture. "You don't do this as a lone wolf. Instead, you coordinate resource management with others as an everyday experience."[22]

Pete Read, a central Oregon rancher with a grazing permit on the Crooked River NG, presented a fascinating case study of this public-private cooperation, speaking at the Fiftieth Anniversary National Grasslands Forum, June 19–22, 1989, at Bismarck, North Dakota. His family had settled the ranch, now adjacent to the grassland, in 1861. Bluebunch wheatgrass then was "belly high on the horse and as far as you could see." There were few juniper trees, only on hilltops or ridges protected from fire. Many of the creeks flowed year round, Read said.

When Read's father was a boy, sagebrush and invasive juniper trees were rapidly replacing the grass, and creeks ran only in the spring. Growing up, Read saw juniper trees and sagebrush everywhere, whereas bluebunch wheatgrass was found only on hills and ridges; creeks ran only after cloud-bursts. Pronghorn were gone and the last sage hen disappeared about 1952. By the 1980s, invasive species were more plentiful than ever, but plowing and reseeding wasn't feasible and "spraying was prohibited." His grazing allotment had declined to 60 percent of carrying capacity.

In desperation, Read presented burning and reseeding plans to the Forest Service, and began burning a pasture each year. Two unforeseen things happened: less than half of the expected area burned, leaving brush and trees for wildlife habitat, and there was more grass left than expected. The next year the entire pasture was circled with fire, leaving 30 to 40 percent of the area untouched, "a nice mosaic pattern for wildlife."

The burning increased forage, but how could it be kept that way? Read had an average grazing period of fifty-four days in four pastures on the Juniper Butte allotment but cattle had overgrazed some areas while leaving other areas untouched or over-rested. That left ideal conditions for more juniper trees and sagebrush. The solution, to start managing for grass, came from Byron Cheney of the Forest Service. By 1989, Read diversified to fourteen pastures instead of four, with an average grazing period per pasture of five to six days, with good results. "We move as the grass grows. If it is growing fast we move fast. If the growth rate slows down we slow our moves down. In each case, we try to avoid grazing any regrowth, giving the grass adequate time to recover," he said. The vigorous grass successfully competes with sagebrush and junipers.

At Juniper Butte today, Read said in 1989, there are unusually high numbers of new seedlings, healthy older plants, and the soil is mellow, with little bare ground. Grazing has become an effective tool, with many cattle cultivating a small area by trampling and compacting the dirt, forming good seed mulch to hold rain in the soil. Cattle also trample and kill sagebrush. Neighboring pastures have no new seedlings and the soil is hard, capped with large bare areas.

"What is best for the grass turns out to be best for the cows," Read said. With the old fifty-four-day grazing period, nutritional levels started high but dropped rapidly; with short five- to six-day periods, cows are always moving to good feed. Calf weaning weights increased 19 percent the first year and calving periods were reduced by almost thirty days. Cows came back to the home ranch in better condition, with higher pregnancy rates than nearby allotments. There was full grazing even under drought conditions, with grass left on the pastures. Read also cared for riparian areas by fencing them, relocated other water supplies for better cattle distribution, and began grazing areas that were untouched before.

"Yes," Read said, "some of the creeks are flowing now—one, year-round with native rainbow trout in it. The antelope are back and doing very well and I hope someday in the near future I will see the sage hen also return to the Crooked River National Grasslands."[23]

II. A GUIDE TO THE NATIONAL GRASSLANDS

Grasslands in the United States and Canada

0   400 miles

Labels on map:

Grasslands National Park

PACIFIC NORTHWEST REGION

NORTHERN REGION

Crooked Lake

Little Missouri

Cedar River

Sheyenne

Grand River

Butte Valley

Curlew

Thunder Basin

Fort Pierre

Buffalo Gap

Oglala

INTERMOUNTAIN REGION

ROCKY MOUNTAIN REGION

Pawnee

PACIFIC SOUTHWEST REGION

Comanche

Cimarron

Kiowa

Rita Blanca

Black Kettle

SOUTHWESTERN REGION

McClellan Creek

SOUTHERN REGION

Caddo

Lyndon B. Johnson

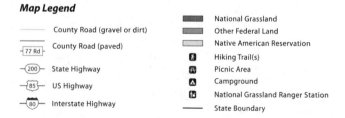

Map Legend

County Road (gravel or dirt)	
County Road (paved) 77 Rd	
State Highway 200	
US Highway 85	
Interstate Highway 80	

National Grassland
Other Federal Land
Native American Reservation

Hiking Trail(s)
Picnic Area
Campground
National Grassland Ranger Station

State Boundary

An Abundance Of Sage Hens

There are still no sage hens (the local name for sage grouse) on the Crooked River NG in central Oregon, as rancher Pete Read wanted, but by mid-2004 they are widespread throughout all the other ranger districts of the Ochoco National Forest and there are about four hundred sage grouse on the Curlew NG in southeast Idaho. In fact, the national grasslands all have abundant wildlife and are natural reserves where the public can view and enjoy native flora and fauna year-round.

The grasslands serve as a valuable treasure house of the natural world, with professional wildlife managers following detailed multiple-use management plans to foster native species, especially those in trouble. There are also several programs designed to reintroduce endangered species into their native habitat on various grasslands.

The U.S. Forest Service has a chief administrator and five deputy chiefs including one for the grasslands. There are nine Forest Service regions, each headed by a regional forester, and national grasslands are in seven of them. Within the regions, each national forest (including, sometimes, a national grassland) has a forest supervisor, with the basic line unit of administration being a district ranger, in charge of one or more individual grasslands, or in some cases half of a larger grassland. Each district ranger works with staff at a ranger station.

National Grasslands Visitor Center

The National Grasslands Visitor Center is in Wall, South Dakota, two blocks from world-famous Wall Drug, and adjoins the Wall District Ranger Station of the Buffalo Gap NG. The center focuses on interpreting the history and natural history of the national grasslands with eighteen permanent exhibits. There are six movies about the grasslands, the badlands, and the Black Hills region, shown in a comfortable theater. An orientation room has maps, more exhibits, an information desk, and book and gift sales. The Wall district station administers the center with one full-time employee, supplemented by another worker in the peak tourist season.

Following is a description of all twenty national grasslands, plus the Grasslands National Park of Canada, Saskatchewan.

Western States Grasslands

In the West, three national grasslands have a variety of wildlife. All three are similar in climate to the Great Plains grasslands, with semiarid prairies brought on by the rain shadow of the Cascade Mountains, just as the Rockies affect the Great Plains.

Crooked River National Grassland

Crooked River NG, in Jefferson County, Oregon, is 111,571 acres of "rolling grasslands and sagebrush-juniper plant communities," according to an official release. There are "nearly lava plains" on the west, sloping to high desert topography with isolated buttes and ridges to the east.[1] Major animal species here include pronghorn, mule deer, Rocky Mountain elk, and mountain lions. Birds include mountain quail, burrowing owls, Canada geese, California quail, great blue heron, meadowlark, horned lark, and great horned

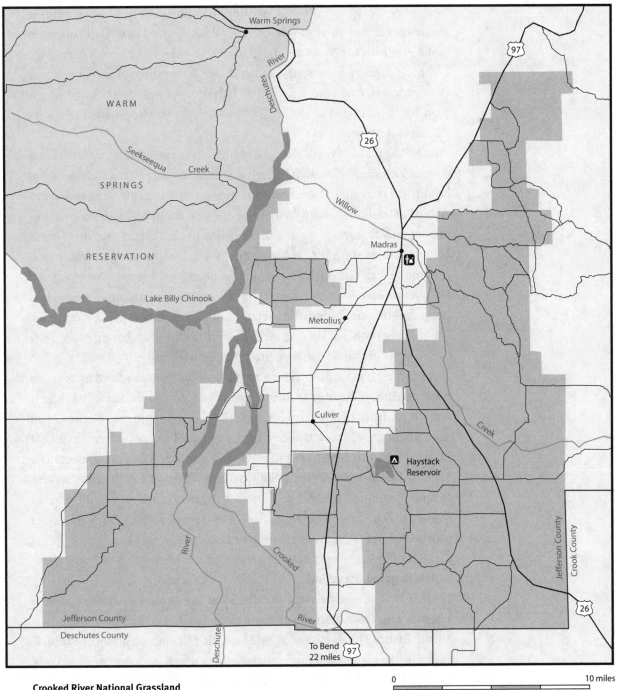

Crooked River National Grassland

0   10 miles

owls. There have been possible sightings of a rare pygmy rabbit, according to Kristin M. Bail, district ranger. The rabbit resembles a small cottontail rabbit, but with a brown tail. The grassland flora includes bunch grass, sagebrush, big sagebrush, western juniper, Idaho fescue, blue bunch grass, crested wheatgrass, rock spirea, arrowleaf balsamroot, and the National Champion Big Sagebrush, the nation's largest such plant. The grassland's ranger station is at Madras.

Bail notes that the grassland is an island within surrounding communities that are growing in human population, with many county roads, power lines, heightened recreational use, and areas used for hunting-dog trials with planted birds. Deschutes County, adjoining the grassland, had a 46 percent population growth between 1990 and 2000, one of the highest rates in Oregon. There are "now more and more people" using the grassland for recreation year-round, Bail said, including mountain biking, off-highway vehicle use on a thousand-acre dedicated area, camping and hiking, and new uses such as "geocache" treasure hunts using satellite-siting instruments. Trash dumping is a growing problem. It is for these reasons that officials have not yet determined if the grassland can support a sage grouse habitat, Bail said.[2]

The biggest habitat problem is a 150 percent juniper woodland increase on the grassland, reducing sagebrush and grassland stands. Crews use chainsaws to control the juniper trees, but "they keep popping up all over," Bail said. There are also controlled fires, using "cool burns" rather than "hot burns" that work best to kill junipers but also devastate the grasses. The grassland's latest environmental impact statement calls for leaving "a greater diversity of grass stubble heights (2–15 inches) at the end of the grazing season. . . . This would help establish deep-rooted native grass species and provide habitat for ground-nesting birds."[3]

Curlew National Grassland

There is also growing tourist popularity at the smaller Curlew NG, 47,658 acres in southeast Idaho near the Utah border. The ranger station is at Malad, Idaho. The grassland is listed on the National Register of Historic Places as it contains the site of a major campsite and stopover on an old trail, Hudspeth's Cutoff, established during the California Gold Rush in 1849. The

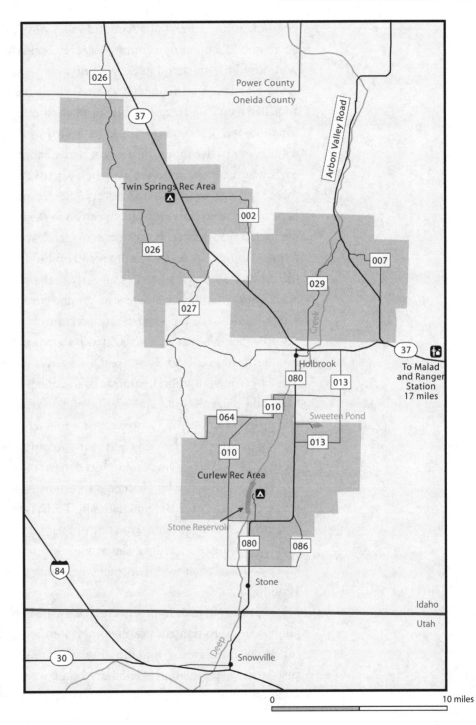

Curlew National Grassland

0   10 miles

grassland is in the heart of a semiarid valley running from Snowville, Utah, north into Idaho to Roy Summit, near the Oneida-Power county line, with portions of the grassland in each county.

The grassland was mainly purchased during the Depression from Idaho and Utah banks who acquired title through foreclosures.[4] Much of it (thirty-five thousand acres) was reseeded to crested wheatgrass and Ladak alfalfa, with "about twelve thousand acres of native range that have not been treated. Sagebrush, bitterbrush, serviceberry, native grasses and forbs occupy these areas," according to one history.[5] Reseeding was also done with bulbous bluegrass in the 1940s. "It is a cousin to the typical lawn grass," according to Rick VanBebber, rangeland manager, "except it tolerates a very arid setting and reproduces by rhizomes and bulbs." However, the grass—much like crested wheatgrass—comes up early in the spring then "dies back and burns back to nothing, so there is no ground cover for bird habitat and little forage value. It was for stopgap erosion control."

VanBebber said that a relatively new program was initiated to rehabilitate two thousand grassland acres a year, with a regime of a prescribed burn followed by tilling the ground, summer fallow, tilling again, then planting wheat, to take the bluegrass out.[6] However, by mid-2004, scarce money had reduced that program to two single projects of a 700-acre burn and a 1,100-acre reseeding treatment in the past eight years, according to Ken Timothy, a wildlife biologist. The reseeding project was done in 1998–99, and in five years the land returned to native bird habitat production. Now the range development plan is to let sagebrush develop naturally. This has produced ideal habitat for sage grouse, leaving the grassland one of their best spots in Idaho. The grassland sage grouse count is 157 males in 2004, with a high of 177 in 1999 and the lowest count of 70 in 1998. The total sage grouse count in 2004 is about 400, Timothy said.

Also present in high numbers are sharp-tailed grouse, enough for a trapping program to reintroduce the birds elsewhere, plus pheasants, curlew, ruff grouse, blue grouse, and other upland bird species. The gray (Hungarian) partridge population is enough to support an annual, lottery hunting season for twenty-five licenses. The grassland is also home to golden and bald eagles, a variety of hawks including marsh hawks using small wetlands, and Canada geese. Larger mammals include deer, elk, bobcats, an occasional mountain lion, and coyotes.[7]

Before 1970 sharp-tailed grouse were not observed in Curlew Valley but today they are common, along with pheasants and partridges, because of twenty-five miles of added windbreaks. Enhancement of Sweeten Pond has improved Canada goose and duck habitat, with fifty geese, four hundred ducks, and several hundred shore birds produced annually.

Fall hunting attracts large numbers of people to the grasslands, as does Stone Reservoir, a privately developed lake for irrigation surrounded by the grassland. There is a campground for recreation vehicles as well as tenting at the reservoir and another campground at Twin Springs on the unit's north end. These and other activities account for as many as seventeen thousand recreation visitor days annually.[8]

Rick VanBebber said that among the plants causing wildlife habitat and forage problems are the invasive leafy spurge and an array of knapweed. Early settlers brought dyer's woad plants from England to make blue dye, used by ancient Picts for tattoos, and that is now a weed problem.[9]

Butte Valley National Grassland

Huge flocks of migrating birds make Butte Valley NG, in north-central California near the Oregon border, one of the most unusual grasslands. It is a shrub-steppe habitat, with sandy terraces and dunes, mostly flat land on an elevated (4,200 feet) basin that is the bed of an ancient lake. Before European settlement, the basin supported an estimated six million waterfowl, but after the 1900s dikes and ditches drained much of it and the 1930s' drought and Depression caused widespread farming failure. However, the area still supports an estimated three million migratory waterfowl annually, in peak numbers.

The unit was an 18,425-acre land utilization project that remained as a "purchase unit," subject to disposal after the other L-U land dispersions in 1960. Local public persistence to seek national grassland designation, along with strong support of the local congressional delegation, helped Butte Val-

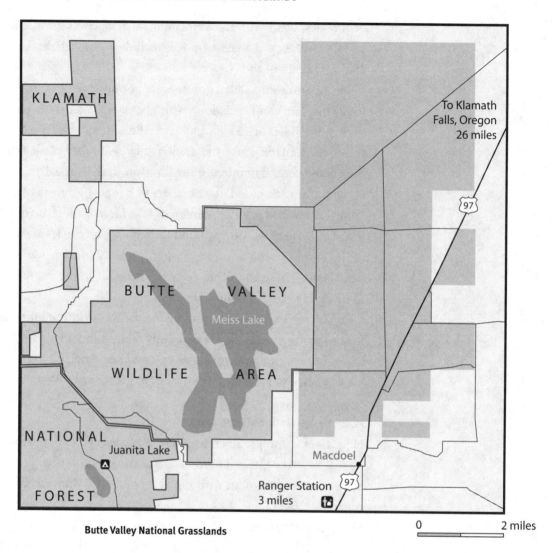

KLAMATH

To Klamath
Falls, Oregon
26 miles

97

BUTTE   VALLEY

Meiss Lake

WILDLIFE   AREA

NATIONAL

Juanita Lake

Macdoel

FOREST

Ranger Station
3 miles

97

Butte Valley National Grasslands

0   2 miles

ley become the newest grassland in 1991. It had previously been considered
as a prison site and county landfill, and in the 1940s was used as a bomb-
ing range. Another 1,280 acres of farmland repossessed by the federal Farm
Home Administration was added in 1994, to make a total of 19,705 acres.
The Butte Valley Wildlife Area, an 11,520-acre reserve administered by the
California Department of Fish and Game, adjoins the grassland and contains shallow Meiss Lake, a 4,000-acre remnant of the ancient lake. There

are spectacular views of the Cascade Range and nearby Mount Shasta.

In past years, spring rains and runoff flooded Meiss Lake and surrounding areas, with excess water pumped into the Klamath River. However, according to Twyla Browning, a range ecologist, the water from the closed basin is naturally alkaline with high water tables and hardpan soil twelve to forty inches below the surface. The perched water tables pull the alkali up to the surface and this caused major pollution problems and fish kills when water was pumped into the river.[10] In 1992 a four-phase wetland development project was initiated to bring vernal wetlands back to the grassland and was successfully completed by 2000. However, three years of drought meant that by mid-2004 the wetlands again disappeared and Meiss Lake itself is dry part of the year, according to Jim Stout, resource officer.[11]

There is still plenty of habitat for wildlife, however, including several bird species that have been listed by the Forest Service as sensitive, such as Swainson's hawks, golden and bald eagles, burrowing owls, short-eared and long-eared owls, merlins, and greater sandhill cranes. In all, 108 bird species have been identified on the grassland and 200 species on the adjoining wildlife area. Among the mammals on the grassland are mule deer, pronghorn, coyote, California ground squirrel, kangaroo rat, marmot, weasel, porcupine, and bobcat. Reptiles include the pygmy horned lizard, California red-sided garter snake, Pacific gopher snake, western rattlesnake, sagebrush lizard, and western fence lizard.

Among the 137 species of vegetation observed on the grassland, the best forage and wildlife habitat are wild rye, Idaho fescue, and Thurber's needle grass, Browning said. Crested wheatgrass was reseeded in the 1950s and is still present. Juniper is the only tree, while shrubs include big sage, black greasewood, spiny hopsage, gray and green rabbitbrush, and bitterbrush. Other forbs and grasses include cheatgrass, salt grass, and Sandberg's bluegrass, according to a report by Jay Carlisle, wildlife biologist.[12]

There are no public facilities on the grassland or the adjoining state wildlife area, but gravel and paved roads provide for windshield tours on ninety square miles of wildlife viewing. About three hundred head of cattle are grazed on the grassland, from May 15 to October 15, about half the normal allotment because of the drought.

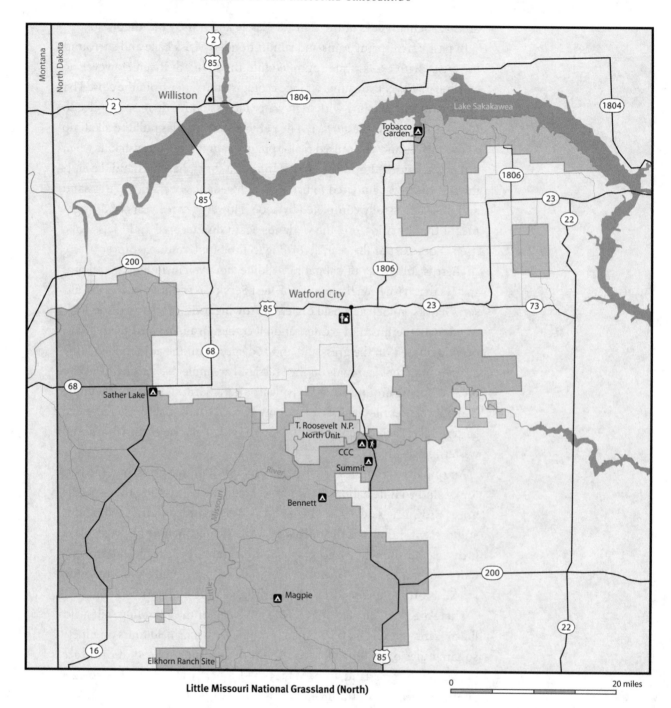

Little Missouri National Grassland (North)

18. One of the most varied grasslands, Comanche National Grassland, located in southeast Colorado, boasts 275 species of birds, dinosaur tracks, and spectacular canyon views.

19. Indian pictograph, Comanche National Grassland

20. Cimarron National Grassland in southwest Kansas

Northern Great Plains Grasslands

Eight national grasslands in the four Northern Great Plains states of North Dakota, South Dakota, Wyoming, and Nebraska, make up the largest amount of grasslands in acres. They also have the most extensive mineral leasing, for coal, oil, gas, and coal-bed natural gas wells. That means heavy infrastructures of roads, power lines, railroads, storage tanks, compressors, large trucks, and huge draglines intruding on the prairie grasslands and their wildlife. They also helped produce $71 million in mineral revenue in 2001 from grassland royalties to the U.S. treasury.

Little Missouri National Grassland

The largest grassland, at 1,028,051 acres, is Little Missouri NG, with two units and ranger districts in western North Dakota. The McKenzie (northern) ranger district station is at Watford City and the Medora (southern) ranger station is at Dickinson. There are about fifty staff members employed by the grassland, with an annual budget approaching two million dollars. The grassland surrounds the Theodore Roosevelt National Park, also in two units, north and south.

An unusual grassland feature is a ninety-seven-mile dirt and gravel trail connecting both districts and the national park, used for horseback riding, mountain biking, and hiking. The Maah Daah Hey multiple-use trail starts up north at a CCC campground twenty miles south of Watford City, off Highway 85, and ends at Sully Creek State Park, south of Medora, a popular tourist town. The trail's name is from the Mandan Indians and means, approximately, "old trail that will always be there."

There is spectacular scenery in the grassland, especially the tall, highly dissected badlands that extend up to five miles from the Little Missouri River that borders the area. This broken-up land has tall buttes, woody draws, and juniper hillsides with important wildlife habitat for deer, turkey, sharp-tailed grouse, and the spotted towhee. Moody Plateau supports a large bighorn sheep herd of about two hundred animals, which were reintroduced in 1956. Elk have also been reintroduced. There are many songbird species, among an estimated two hundred bird species observed in the grassland,

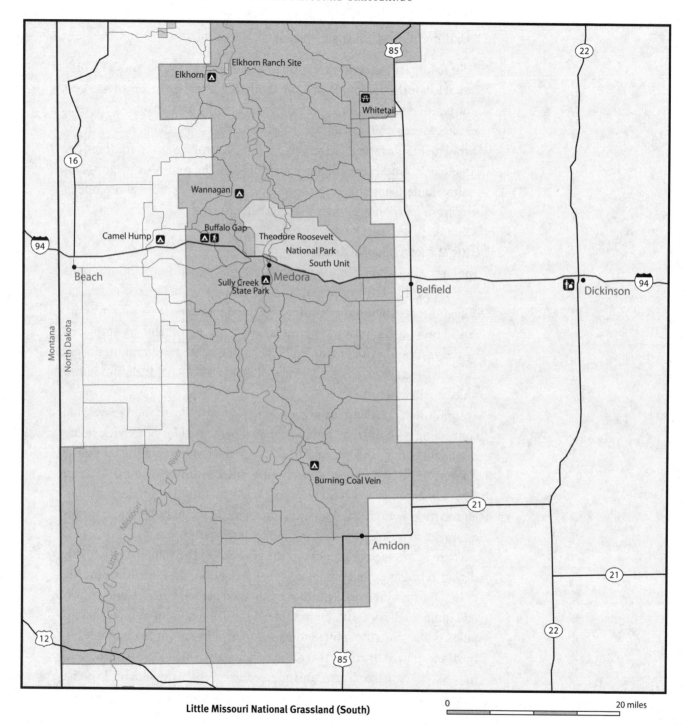

Little Missouri National Grassland (South)

0   20 miles

according to Gary Foli, wildlife biologist in the McKenzie district.

Foli reports that wolves are seen infrequently on the grassland and bison wander out of the Theodore Roosevelt National Park, which has a herd of about two hundred. The bison are chased back into the park or, less frequently, are shot, as the grassland does not have a bison allotment. Other major grassland species include pronghorn, coyotes, bobcats, an occasional mountain lion, golden eagles, prairie falcons, Baird's sparrows, sage grouse, Hungarian partridges, large flocks of migratory waterfowl, warblers, plus an occasional migrating whooping crane.

Foli said the river bottom and adjoining badlands make up the more spectacular landscape, but most of the grassland is rolling prairie with some unusual scoria formations. These are clay knobs where coal deposits burned and melted the clay, leaving a hard surface that remains when the surrounding soil is eroded. The material is sometimes used to surface roads in the grassland.

The mid-grass prairie features about 10 percent crested wheatgrass with some invasive Kentucky bluegrass and leafy spurge also found. The preferred foliage, however, is western wheat and needle grasses for cattle forage and wildlife cover. The Forest Service plan calls for grass stubble height to be left in a high structure after grazing, and this is measured by Robel poles, tall poles with inch-wide colored bands to indicate desired grass height. There are green ash, cottonwood, and elm trees in wooded draws, with ponderosa pine and mountain juniper on the buttes.

Fire fighters have been added to the grassland staff even though most wild fires are of short duration, although a 1999 Halloween fire from Wyoming, fed by fifty-mile-per-hour winds, burned ninety thousand acres. There are some controlled fires in crested wheatgrass areas and underground coal seams sometimes burn and fire pops up to the surface.

Public facilities are excellent on the grassland and the park, with many campgrounds, especially along the Maah Daah Hey Trail. About 560 miles of paved roads are maintained by county and oil company crews, plus many miles of two-track dirt roads that allow windshield tours throughout the huge grassland. A new scenic interpretive site above the river, Burnt Hills Overlook, commemorates a Lewis and Clark Expedition event where Meriwether Lewis was shot in the buttocks by one of his men and nearly died. George Custer and his soldiers passed through the grassland in May 1876, en route to their fate at Little Big Horn, Montana.

Campgrounds have potable water, picnic grounds, camping pads, toilets, and even a metered shower. Ten-acre Sather Lake has camping and allows boating with electric motors or canoes. There are more than 750 archaeological sites on the grassland, plus petrified Giant Sequoia tree stumps along roads, Foli said.

Private land intersperses the public grassland acres and there is heavy cattle grazing throughout with 253 allotments in the Medora district and more than 190 allotments in the McKenzie district. Together the districts allow permits for about forty-two thousand head of cattle, but actual numbers were reduced by about 20 percent in 2004 because of the drought. There are more than five hundred producing oil wells on the grassland and there may be even more activity because of higher oil prices, according to Foli. Natural gas is flared off unless there is enough concentration to establish pipelines. There are no coal mines.

The combination of tourist activities in Medora, state parks and facilities, the national park, and new interest in the Lewis and Clark Expedition means that visits to the grassland are increasing greatly. Year-round activities include cross-country skiing, hunting, camping, biking, and hiking, along with off-road vehicle use of dirt tracks.[13]

Sheyenne River National Grassland

The biggest tallgrass-prairie grassland is the Sheyenne River NG, at nearly seventy-one thousand acres in southeast North Dakota, with the district ranger station at Lisbon. It is very diverse, with eight different habitat types, a threatened wild orchid, some 280 species of birds, and two rare butterfly species.

The Sheyenne River, with river bottom woods of green ash and elm, borders the grassland. There is a choppy sand hills area along the river with high-relief dunes that are an estimated twelve thousand years old, and second-growth trees along the north aspect of the dunes, according to Curt Hansen, a range conservationist. They are part of the Sheyenne Delta,

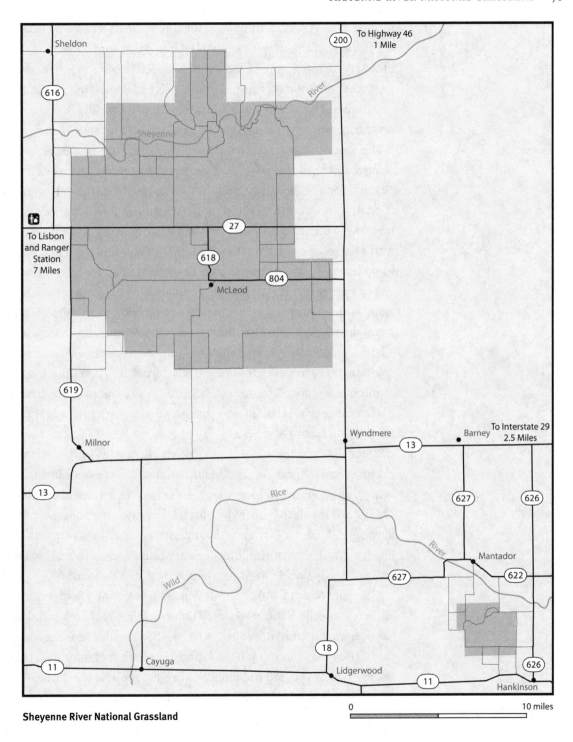

Sheyenne River National Grassland

0   10 miles

formed from glacial meltwater, carved out of the riverbed, and deposited on the east side of the river. Other habitat types are twenty-five thousand acres of tallgrass prairie, one of the nation's largest existing remnants; wetlands or swales and potholes formed from a perched water table of sand overlaid on silts and clays from a glacial lake twenty-five to fifty-feet deep; an oak savannah; aspen parkland; mixed-grass prairie; and river terraces.[14]

The Sheyenne provides habitat for two rare butterfly species, the Dakota skipper and regal fritillary. The threatened western prairie white-fringed orchid has "one of the largest populations known to exist" on the grassland.[15] It occurs "most often in remnant native prairies," wet prairies, and sedge meadows, according to a bulletin. It is a "stout, erect, long-lived perennial with a showy open raceme (spike) of up to two dozen white to creamy white bisymmetric flowers often an inch or more in size."[16]

Bird species include a breeding population of the greater prairie chicken, along with turkeys, loons, white pelicans, several types of grebes, whistling, swans, herons, and egrets, many species of ducks and geese, and cormorants. A large complex of beavers inhabits ponds along the river, along with fairly common occurrences of moose and elk, coyote, fox, porcupine, many types of mice, voles, and shrews, deer, bobcats, mink, and badgers. Bryan Stotts, district ranger, said that on very rare occasions, bears and wolves come into the grassland from Minnesota.

Stotts also said there is a variety of exotic grasses in the unit that present problems for grazing and wildlife habitat. These especially include leafy spurge, plus Kentucky bluegrass, Canadian thistle, brome, and other species. These are difficult to control by burning because ten thousand cattle graze in the grassland, on fifty-three allotments, and pastures cannot be burned, tilled, and rested to control the invasive weeds. "We are overstocked but [we are] politically unable to adjust them downward," he said.[17]

A 25-mile North Country Trail winds through the grassland, a portion of the 3,200-mile National Scenic Trail from New York to North Dakota. It has been rebuilt and moved to better locations, with gravel, new signs, and new self-closing gates. It is used for horseback riding, mountain bikes, and hiking. Winter uses are snowmobiling and cross-country skiing. A favorite fall activity is viewing the colorful autumn foliage.

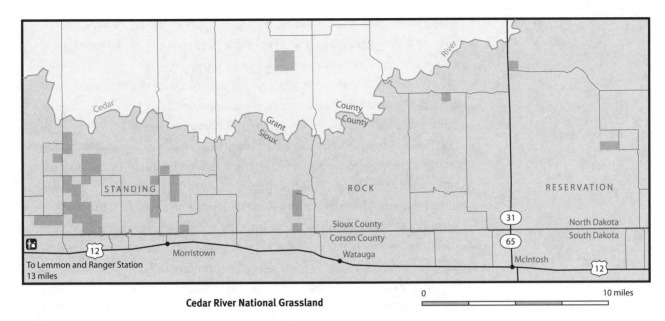

Cedar River National Grassland

Another trail, an eight-mile loop, is in the separate southeast portion of the grasslands, Hankinson Hills, with a new campground at the trailhead.

Cedar River National Grassland

The last North Dakota grassland is the smallest and most scattered of the Northern Great Plains grasslands. Cedar River NG is 6,960 acres, almost all within Standing Rock Reservation of the Lakota Sioux. There is a block of acres along the South Dakota border, just east of Lemmon, South Dakota, where the district ranger station is located; the remaining acres are scattered in blocks further east, in Grant and Sioux Counties, North Dakota.

Administration of this grassland is combined with the much larger Grand River NG just over the border in South Dakota, with a staff of four at Lemmon. Cedar River Grassland is within a half mile of the Cedar River, but there are no river bottomlands included. The topography is all gently rolling prairie, with a few small buttes or hills, all in grassland, intersected by streams and dry gullies. Soils are heavy clays with some gumbo and sandy loam.

Bob Anderson, range technician, said the grassland is about 25 percent crested wheatgrass from prior reseeding, supporting whitetail deer, prong-horn, and sharp-tailed grouse. There are pheasants, though these game birds prefer the nearby cultivated fields.

There are few developed roads, mainly two-track dirt prairie roads and no public facilities. Visitors come to see the birds and hunt in the fall. Some 1,150 head of cattle graze on eleven allotments to ranchers.[18]

Potholes, known locally as glory holes, and small stock ponds support waterfowl, especially gadwall, blue-winged teal, and mallard ducks, accord-ing to wildlife biologist Dan Svingen. Other birds observed include high concentrations of western meadowlark, Bairds's sparrow (a sensitive spe-cies with declining numbers), lark bunting, dickcissel, Sprague's pipit, mi-grating red-tailed and ferruginous hawk, Swainson's hawk, northern har-rier, eagle, and American kestrel. There are infrequent beaver and muskrat, several species of mice and voles, and coyotes and foxes to prey on them. There are occasional badgers and long-tailed badgers.

The habitat is fairly simple, Svingen said, because of the small and scat-tered nature of the grassland. Because streams freeze solid in the winter but have roaring torrents in the spring, and are stagnant pools in the summer and fall, they support only the hardy fathead minnow as the dominant fish species. The potholes, however, support seven fish species, painted turtles, and northern leopard frogs, a sensitive species.

While the Baird's sparrow uses the crested wheatgrass habitat, the pre-ferred grasses for wildlife cover and cattle forage are native species such as western wheat needle, needle and thread, green needle, blue grama, and some little bluestem.[19]

There have been battles between tribal officials and the Forest Service over land ownership and exchanges. In some cases they couldn't even agree on where to meet to talk, according to Forest Morin, a range manager.[20] Some forty-eight thousand acres on the Cedar River and Grand River Grasslands came from the Standing Rock Indian Reservation through homesteading, according to one report. "The federal government in the 1930s acquired these lands. About eleven thousand acres were later returned to the tribe; however, the Standing Rock Sioux Tribe has requested that the rest be re-turned as well." This matter must be resolved by congressional action.[21]

Grand River National Grassland

Grand River NG, at 154,200 acres, is much bigger than Cedar River NG and is concentrated in larger blocks of land, interspersed with private lands. There is the same rolling prairie, but buttes are larger with isolated badland features. It is in Perkins and Corson Counties, South Dakota, and adjoins Standing Rock Reservation.

A robust aquatic habitat includes the north and south forks of the Grand River, meeting at Shadehill Dam and Reservoir (comprising eight thou-

Grand River National Grassland

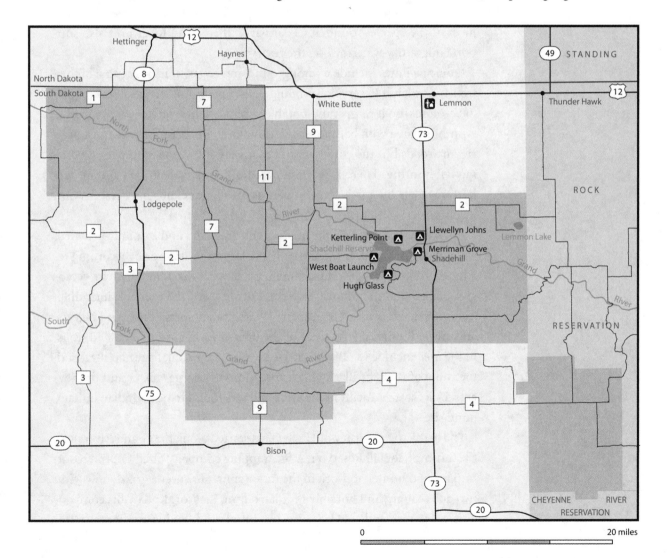

sand acres). The main Grand River flows out of the reservoir and nearby Flat Creek Lake. Game fish such as bass and bluegill are found in the rivers with walleye, northern pike, channel catfish, and yellow perch in the reservoir. There is a fish cleaning area. There are river bottom areas with wooded draws of green ash, box elder, and American elm trees plus chokecherry and buffalo berry shrubs. Mixed native grasses are found on the flat prairies and Robel poles are used to determine desired stubble height for cattle grazing.

There are prairie dog towns on the grassland, supporting a mixture of predators and birds such as burrowing owls, a sensitive species. Besides most of the species found at Cedar River, the Grand River unit also supports migratory waterfowl on the reservoir.

Public facilities include a campground and recreation area with a hiking trail at Shadehill Reservoir, camping pads, toilets, hot showers, several picnic grounds, boat ramps, and potable running water. There is a designated swimming area with bathhouses. The majority of roads are two-track prairie dirt roads but the county gravel roads are heavily used, especially during fall hunting. There is no designated off-road vehicle area and motorized travel off the roads is forbidden, as on all grasslands in Forest Service Region 1.[22]

Petrified wood is found throughout the grassland and a unique petrified wood park in Lemmon is reportedly the largest in the world, according to a local publication. O. S. Quammen, an area pioneer and amateur geologist, helped find mammoth bones and other fossilized remains, including leaves and grass blades. Quammen gathered many sorts of petrified objects and erected unusual structures of the items in a Lemmon park. Old trails in the area include the Bismarck-Deadwood stage trail, begun in 1877, and the route of the 1874 Black Hills expedition of George Custer and the Seventh U.S. Cavalry. A cliff in the grassland was found to be an Indian buffalo jump site.

The heroic 1823 journey of Hugh Glass started along the Grand River near the future Shadehill Reservoir. A fur trapping company hired Glass, a scout, trapper, and hunter, to work in the mountains. However a grizzly sow with two cubs caught and horribly mutilated him. Left for dead by his companions, he revived and crawled some two hundred miles in two months to Ft.

Kiowa, a trading post. It is one of the most remarkable odysseys in Western American history. A monument in his honor has been erected near the reservoir.[23]

Fort Pierre National Grassland

Numerous endangered and sensitive species are found at Fort Pierre NG, with more than 116,000 acres in south-central South Dakota. Highway 83, soon to be a four-lane expressway, bisects the grassland; otherwise there are only gravel roads and two-track dirt roads with no developed public facilities. The grassland is west of the Lower Brule Indian Reservation and the Missouri River. It is south of Pierre, the state capital.

The terrain is rolling mixed and mid-grass prairie with eight intermittent creeks and about four hundred potholes and stock ponds with dams. The ponds are fisheries with bass, black bullhead, and pan fish and are fairly heavily used. Two ponds, the sixteen-acre Richland Wildlife Area and the twenty-one-acre pond at Sheriff's Dam, are fenced to keep livestock out, and people often make primitive camps there. Scattered trees along the creek bottoms include plains cottonwood, sandbar and peach willows, and green ash. There also are Rocky Mountain juniper trees.

The native grasses are western wheatgrass, needle-and-thread grass, buffalo grass, blue and sideoats grama, porcupine grass, and big and little bluestem. Exotic species partially controlled by herbicides are Canadian thistle and sickle weed, which has invaded in the past ten years. A South Dakota State University range specialist is experimenting with herbicides to eliminate the sickle weed, a member of the carrot family that tends to take over pastures and compete with forage and habitat cover grasses. Prescribed burns are used in springtime to get rid of excessive ground litter and to give native species a chance to outdo the invaders, according to wildlife biologist Glenn Moravek.

Migrating whooping cranes and bald eagles are endangered species observed at the grassland. Sensitive species include the black-tailed prairie dog, grass sparrow, short-eared owl, burrowing owl, American bittern, ferruginous hawk, greater prairie chicken, chestnut-collared longspur (which nests on the ground), loggerhead shrike, long-billed curlew, eastern screech

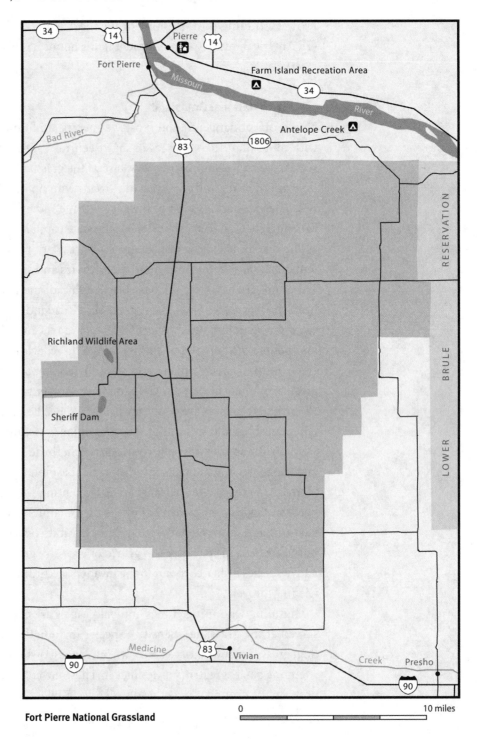

Fort Pierre National Grassland

0   10 miles

owl, ruby-throated hummingbird, willow flycatcher, regal fritillary butterfly, and the northern leopard frog.

Other flora on the grassland include western snowberry shrubs scattered on the creek bottoms. There are two hundred bird species observed on the grassland including sharp-tailed grouse, pheasant, grasshopper sparrow, dickcissel, upland sandpiper, marbled godwit (a shore bird), American white pelican, and western meadowlark. Larger mammals include mule and whitetail deer, pronghorn, coyotes, and other animals typical of a mixed-grass prairie. Blinds are available for public use to watch springtime courtship rituals of prairie chickens and sharp-tailed grouse on their dancing grounds.

The endangered swift fox has been released from the nearby Bad Rivers Ranches, owned by Ted Turner, and radio signals from their collars indicate they are on the grassland. The Turner Endangered Species Fund, providing two wildlife biologists on the ranches, is planning to release more swift fox on the grassland. Moravek said there is close cooperation between Forest Service and Turner staff.

The swift fox is the rarest wild dog in North America, according to a report. It has short speeds of thirty-five miles per hour. Once plentiful on the Midwestern prairies, the animal was extirpated from Canada and has drastically declined elsewhere. Reintroduction efforts began in the 1980s and today a small but stable population exists in the Great Plains. The swift fox's chief enemy is the coyote who will kill, often without eating them, just to get rid of them. A nocturnal hunter, the swift fox "feeds on mice, moles, crickets, ground squirrels and other small prey, as well as berries and seeds. . . . When its fur is wet, a swift fox looks no bigger than a large house cat." They have a year-round underground lifestyle, changing burrows frequently.[24]

The grassland staff includes nine people during the summer and five full-time staffers in the winter. There is one grazing association with thirty-one members, plus six individual cattle grazing permitees. About 51,500 units per month are allowed from May to October on 210 pastures, with some winter grazing allowed. There are no mineral or oil and gas leases on the grassland.[25]

The grassland has had a bison permit on two allotments of 4,880 acres since 1996. Rod Sather bought a ranch that had permits and has put 203 bison cows and 24 bison bulls on the pastures. The Forest Service is allowing winter grazing, so the bison are on the grassland from June 1 to the first week of January. The bison forage on western wheatgrass, big bluestem, and some buffalo grass, according to Tonya Weisbeck, range conservationist.[26]

Buffalo Gap National Grassland

Buffalo Gap NG in southwest South Dakota is one of the more diverse of the prairie grasslands, and at 596,917 acres in two units is the second largest grassland. It has a very successful reintroduction program for the black-footed ferret, probably the most endangered North American mammal, and has plant and animal species listed as sensitive.

A ranger station at Wall, South Dakota, administers the grassland's eastern unit, reaching to Interstate 90. The National Grasslands Visitor Center adjoins the district headquarters and is administered by district officials. The Fall River Ranger Station for the western unit, extending to the Nebraska border, is at Hot Springs. The grassland surrounds much of the Badlands National Park and adjoins Pine Ridge Indian Reservation. The Black Hills National Forest is nearby; Angastura Reservoir, a state recreation area with cabins, camping, boating, and a marina is within ten miles; and huge Custer State Park is close, with herds of bison and elk and well-developed tourist facilities including lodges, campgrounds, trails, and picnic areas. A diversity of habitats on the grassland includes tall-, mixed-, and shortgrass prairie; woody draws; many wetlands and stock ponds; rivers; and badland formations.

The grassland is one of the most concentrated, because many of the diverse, checkerboard units have been consolidated by trading land with nearby ranchers. In fact, in the Nebraska National Forest region that includes Oglala, Fort Pierre, and Buffalo Gap NGs, there have been about 135,000 acres in trades since 1986. A second generation of ranchers is beginning the process again, with ten to twelve land exchange proposals for some ten thousand acres being processed in 2004. Blocking up the land provides more efficient operations for private ranches and more successful multiple

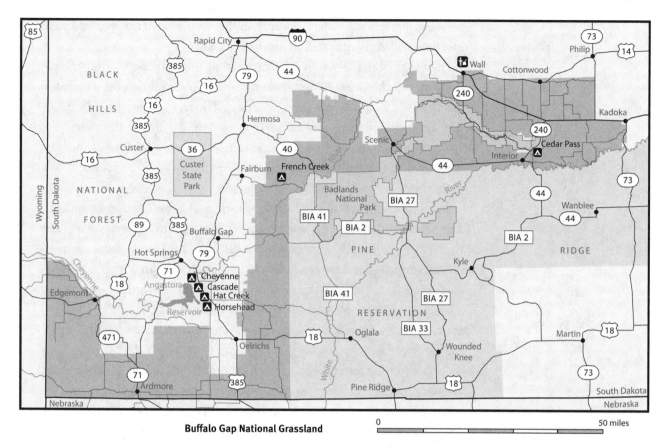

Buffalo Gap National Grassland

0   50 miles

use and wildlife management on the grasslands, according to Bill Perry, district ranger. The land exchanges are not on an acreage basis but are value-for-value, depending on equal land assessments.

The black-footed ferret reintroduction project on the Wall District is the most successful of twelve such programs across the Great Plains and in Mexico. Biologists released 151 kits on the grassland and by 2003 there was a recorded population of 263, meaning that the ferrets are reproducing naturally into second and third generations, Perry said. The staff spent six months tracking coyotes—the chief enemy of the ferrets—and then placed the ferrets in coyote-free areas. "We even tracked one coyote to Sturgis and back; it was like someone put him in a car and drove him there," more than a hundred miles, Perry said. In the other twelve reintroduction sites, the recovered ferrets were many fewer than the number originally introduced and had almost disappeared in some projects.[27]

The range of the ferret, formerly spread throughout eight hundred million acres of the Great Plains, depends upon three prairie dog species for food and shelter, according to one report. The ferrets were feared extinct until a ranch dog in Wyoming killed one in 1981, leading to discovery of a colony of 130 animals in 1984. Disease caused the population to dwindle to eighteen and these were captured and bred so they could be reintroduced to the wild.

Black-footed ferrets are nocturnal, mostly living underground in prairie dog towns, and spend only a few minutes above ground per day. They are the size of a mink, up to three pounds full-grown, with long slender bodies and short legs and are generally yellowish buff in color with black feet, a black mask, and black tail tip. Prairie dogs, about the same size as the ferrets, are attacked at the neck and a desperate struggle ensues. The ferrets also eat mice, squirrels, rabbits, birds, and "even reptiles and insects," according to the report.[28]

A black-footed ferret had been kept in a room at the Wall office to show visitors, especially ranchers who often became convinced of the need to preserve prairie dog habitat on the grassland after seeing the frisky, beautiful animal. The display ferret was rotated back to the wild every few months.

Swift fox, also rare, were released in the Badlands National Park and were later recorded on the Wall unit with a couple of dens a year observed. Other sensitive species, according to Bob Hodorff, wildlife biologist, include big-eared and fringed myotis bats, and the northern leopard frog, common on the grassland. Fish include the plains minnow, sturgeon chub, and pearl and fine dace. The pearl dace is found in the Cheyenne River, which flows through the grassland. There is Barr's milk vetch, a rare plant discovered on the grassland by Claude Barr, and Dakota buckwheat, both listed as sensitive plants. Barr collected more than 1,400 plant species during sixty-five years as a rancher near Smithwick, South Dakota, and they are housed at Chadron State College, Chadron, Nebraska, along with his collection of books, journals, and letters.

Birds on the sensitive list include the grasshopper sparrow (common on

21. Sitting on the border between Oklahoma and Texas, the Rita Blanca National Grassland offers serenity and big sky views.

22. Unique among the national grasslands, Mills Canyon of
New Mexico's Kiowa National Grassland provides a habitat
sanctuary for a host of creatures including Barbary sheep.

the grassland), short-eared and burrowing owl, American bittern and black tern (at large stock ponds), ferruginous hawk, McCown's and chestnut-collared longspur, sage grouse (none seen since 2003), mountain plover, northern harrier, yellow-billed cuckoo (along the Cheyenne River), trumpeter swan (breeding at the nearby Lacreek National Wildlife Refuge), peregrine falcon, loggerhead shrike (found in woody draws), long-billed curlew, and Brewer's sparrow (in sagebrush). Two sensitive butterflies are the Ottoe skipper and the regal fritillary.[29] Checklists show 114 wildlife species, more than 230 bird species, 47 grasses, and 199 wildflower and tree species.

There are good gravel roads throughout the grassland, plus two-track prairie roads, and paved state and federal highways. There is a developed Pioneer Rest Area on Highway 385, north of the Nebraska border, with wetlands, picnic area, and toilet. A campground is on French Creek, east of Fairburn on Custer County Road 18, with fire grates, toilet, and picnic tables, but no potable water.

There are three grazing associations on the Fall River District, with one hundred thousand animal unit months (AUMS) permitted, and twenty-five thousand to thirty thousand head of cattle. Many types of management are used, including time control grazing that has short-term, high intensity use. Mike Erk, a range conservationist, said there was a decade in the 1990s of "wonderful" weather with plenty of rain and bountiful pastures. A drought starting in 2001, however, reduced forage to one-quarter of its normal production by 2004 and cattle grazing was down considerably. "Some areas never greened up at all," in the spring of 2004, and it was "one of the hardest years since I came here in 1987."[30] Two grazing associations and twenty-four direct permitees have allotments for seventy-thousand AUMS, or fourteen thousand to fifteen thousand head of cattle, on the Wall District, Perry said. Grazing was "pretty tough" in 2004 and "ranchers have made their own cuts" in grazing.[31]

In 1961 Forest Service officials with their management "programs of meticulous control" angered members of the Pioneer, Cottonwood, and Indian Creek grazing associations on the Buffalo Gap NG, according to a historian. Federal delegates met with association delegates in Rapid City at a sometimes clamorous hearing. The associations successfully defended two points, keeping permit contracts at ten years instead of a proposed five years, and the use of "overhead" money, assessments charged to members for legal costs in court battles. These successes prompted the start of the South Dakota Grasslanders Association in 1962 and led to the creation of the Association of National Grassland Associations (now called the Association of National Grasslands) in 1964.[32]

Dan O'Brien, a noted author, had been a cattle rancher in South Dakota who switched to bison and bought a ranch on the Cheyenne River that includes a twenty-thousand-acre winter grazing allotment for bison on the national grassland. He has nearly 300 bison cows, most with calves, and 30 bison bulls on two ranches. He put 110 head of bison on the grassland in 2004. He has installed twenty-six miles of "good bison fence," O'Brien said. The bison will graze during the winter, starting in November. Cattle from other ranchers will graze the pastures during the summer. The area is slated to be part of a 22,700-acre wilderness area, the first such designation on any national grassland, upon congressional approval. That generally means no mechanized or motorized vehicles on the land, and horses will be used to check the bison. O'Brien said it would take two days to check the entire allotment on horseback. He has an electronic online bison meat business, Wild Idea Buffalo Company, which markets frozen bison meat nationally. The bison are "eco-friendly, grass-fed, and pasture-killed," according to O'Brien and it is "the purest, healthiest red meat on the planet."[33] Another bison allotment is held by the Triple 7 Ranch.

Oglala National Grassland

Fossilized bones and toadstool rock formations help make the Oglala NG unique. The grassland, 94,480 acres on Sioux and Dawes Counties, in northwest Nebraska, is part of a "smart tourists" route of attractions in the area. It has typical Dakota rolling prairies and mid- to short grasses, with buttes and extensive badlands that feature heavy clay and Pierre shale soils. The Pine Ridge Escarpment, an extension of the Rocky Mountain environment with ponderosa pine forests, is south of the grassland, and a small segment known as Round Top Butte extends into the grassland. Round Top is a ponderosa pine habitat not typical of grasslands.

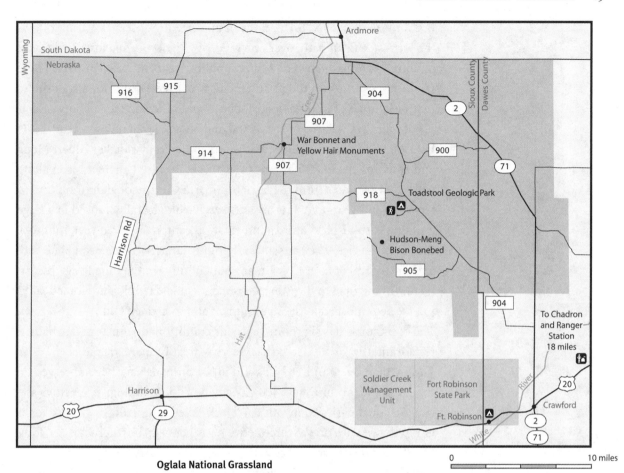

Oglala National Grassland

0   10 miles

The grassland and the Pine Ridge unit of the Nebraska National Forest are administered by the Chadron Ranger District, with a staff of twelve (rising to twenty to twenty-two in the summer) and an annual budget of $750,000 to $900,000, according to Charlie Marsh, district ranger.[34] While there are no developed campgrounds, camping and hiking are allowed anywhere on public lands and there are extensive gravel and dirt roads. Highways 71 and 2 pass through the grasslands from Crawford to the South Dakota border. The Burlington Northern Santa Fe Railroad bisects the grassland.

The grassland surrounds Toadstool Geologic Park, a Forest Service park.

It is a maze of eroded formations in an eerie moonscape. A trail follows the longest known path, over one mile, of Oligocene epic fossilized tracks of animals along the bed of a thirty-million-year-old braided river. There is a campground with toilets and picnic areas; a one-mile loop trail shows many examples of unusual toadstool clay and sandstone formations. A couple of miles away across the grassland, but about eleven miles by road, is the Hudson-Meng Bison Bonebed. It was discovered by rancher Albert Meng and contains the fossil remains of some six hundred ancient bison along with stone artifacts from the ancient Alberta Culture of eight thousand to ten thousand years ago. It is an active archaeological dig housed in a large building with displays and an information center, operated year-round by the Forest Service. The grassland adjoins the large Fort Robinson State Park and the federal Soldier Creek management unit, in the Pine Ridge Escarpment. On the road to the Bonebed is the seasonal High Plains Homestead, a private bed-and-breakfast establishment and re-created Old West cow town. The bunkhouse has six rooms, each air conditioned with a private bath. A restaurant, the Drifter Cookshack, serves great homemade pies.

More than one hundred birds and fifty mammals have been observed on the grassland, according to Jeff Abegglen, wildlife biologist. Sensitive species include the fringed myotis bat, black-tailed prairie dog, swift fox, ferruginous hawk with one to three active nests per year, northern harrier, long-billed curlew with several colonies in pastures, burrowing owl, migrating American peregrine falcon, short-eared owl, loggerhead shrike, McCown's and chestnut-collared longspur, and the northern leopard frog. More common species include mule and whitetail deer, pronghorn, coyote, wild turkey, elk and big horn sheep on Round Top, and sharp-tailed grouse with scattered leks, or dancing grounds.

There are more than one hundred stock ponds and a couple of larger reservoirs on the grassland, built for livestock in the 1930s and 1940s by the Civilian Conservation Corps. Some of these have been fenced out to protect riparian areas, and they are mostly dry in mid-2004 because of the lingering drought, Abegglen said. Normally they hold water year-round. Cottonwood, green ash, and willow trees are found along streams. Forest Service officials imposed limited fire restrictions in 2003 and 2004 on the Oglala and Buffalo Gap Grasslands, banning open fires except in fire pits of developed areas.

Typical native grasses are western wheatgrass and green needle grass. Invasive and noxious plants are Japanese brome, cheatgrass, broom snakeweed, and Canadian thistle. Hand-spraying herbicide on individual plants, rather than broadcast spraying, controls the noxious plants and protects wanted grasses, Abegglen said. They also try to manage the land for shrubs such as silver sage, as habitat for sharp-tailed grouse.[35]

The Sugarloaf Grazing Association has thirty-three members with thirty-five allotments on ninety-five pastures. The Forest Service also has one direct permitee with allotments on both Oglala and Buffalo Gap Grasslands. The Sugarloaf group charges extra fees to members to help maintain an extensive network of plastic pipelines that were first installed in the 1960s, leading to stock tanks in pastures and providing water to ranch headquarters.

Thunder Basin National Grassland

Gas, oil, and coal are the big resources on the 553,287 acres of the Thunder Basin NG in Wyoming, third largest and wealthiest of the national grasslands. There are five major coal mines on the grassland, including Black Thunder, the largest surface coal mine in North America. Another mine produces the most coal tonnage in North America. In fact, according to Bob Sprentall, district ranger for Thunder Basin, about 20 percent of the nation's coal comes from the grassland public lands and intermingled private lands. In 2003 the grassland produced $53 million in mineral leases and royalties for the U.S. Treasury, up from $46 million in 2001.[36]

Total mineral revenue from eight grasslands was $71 million in 2001, according to Bruce Ramsey, a Forest Service official. Of that, 25 to 50 percent was returned to the producing states and/or counties, depending on a complicated formula.[37] That number compares to an average annual revenue of $918,852 from all land utilization projects (11.3 million acres) from 1942 to 1953, including sales of forest products, grazing fees, and mineral royalties.

The eight grasslands currently producing mineral income are Pawnee, Comanche, Cimarron, Kiowa, Black Kettle, Lyndon B. Johnson, Thunder Basin,

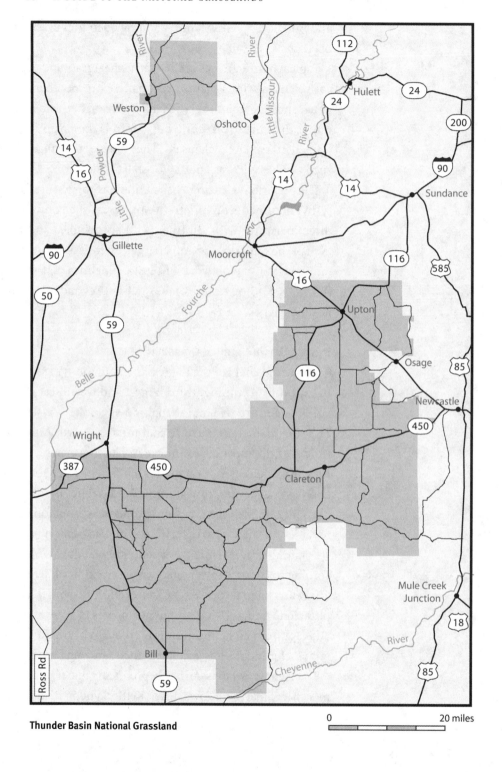

Thunder Basin National Grassland

0   20 miles

and Little Missouri. In 1971 mineral leases on the national grasslands produced $1.4 million, and grazing fee income was $700,000. For the grazing season of 2000–2001, grazing fees dropped to $580,066, then to $471,721 the next year, and were $491,753 in 2002–2003, according to Cecile Gray, of the Forest Service.[38]

Coal produced from Thunder Basin provides 70 percent of all grasslands' mineral revenue, with oil and gas from all eight producing grasslands providing 30 percent. The biggest source of coal revenue, according to Ramsey, comes from one-time bonus bids per acre for coal leases, where the amount of coal is generally known and production is fairly certain. Oil leases are more speculative and depend upon drilling for discovery. In addition, there are yearly mineral royalties of varying amounts.

The open-pit coal mines are in Campbell County on the western portion of Thunder Basin NG, and they are a striking feature of the landscape. There is constant activity of explosions with orange smoke blasting into coal beds, roads crawling with huge trucks, and intensive railroad activity with mile-long coal trains being loaded. Trucks dump loads of coal onto large conveyor belts within a quarter mile of an active prairie dog town, but the animals seem unmindful of the noise and dust.

There are huge hydraulic excavators, graders and scrapers, many roads and railroad tracks, and pipelines leading to tank farms from active oil wells. High-power electrical lines intersect the landscape. Coal-bed natural gas wells need underground pipelines, electric lines, and wellhead compressor stations, with larger compressor stations serving many wells through a web of pipes. The wells are located one per eighty acres and need a huge amount of infrastructure.

All this mining and drilling activity produces huge scars on the grassland, polluting smoke and dust, and unwanted water and pollution from the coal-bed natural gas wells. According to Mary Peterson, forest supervisor, there is a "heavy dust abatement problem" in Campbell County. The dust and activity are affecting mountain plover nests and disturbing sage grouse, burrowing owls, prairie dogs, sharp-tailed grouse, and a wide variety of raptors.

The natural gas is extracted by drilling into the aquifer above the coal bed where the gas is trapped in porous rock. Water is extracted with the gas. The gas goes into pipelines to compressor stations, but the water cannot be reinjected into the ground. On the grassland, ponds are required by the Forest Service to hold the water for evaporation. That is not the case on nearby private lands, however, where water from wells runs into streams. Some of the water may be polluted with heavy metals or it can be highly saline, which sterilizes the soil and kills fish in the Cheyenne River, Peterson said. The state of Wyoming does not test the water quality. If the water is drinkable, ranchers like it because it causes intermittent streams to become permanent streams for better cattle use. However, this changes the arid or semiarid ecosystem to a wet climate, significantly altering the native plant and animal habitat and also presenting road engineering, archaeological, and fossil issues. There are currently two hundred to three hundred coalbed natural gas wells on the grassland but the business is booming now and Peterson expects thousands more wells from pending applications.[39]

Along with the Cheyenne, three other major rivers flow through Thunder Basin National Grassland—the Little Powder River, the Belle Fourche River, and the Little Missouri River, all eventually flowing into the Missouri River. In addition, there are three eastward-facing escarpments, the Rochelle, Red, and Miller Hills, with coal seams lying just to their west. Over the years some of the coal has burned, causing the overlying sandstone to bake into orange and black scoria rock, creating strange conical formations. East of the hills is broken plains grassland, and uplands and benches with colorful badlands of sandstone, shale and mudstone, according to Forest Service information.

The largest concentration of public land in the grassland is in the western portion, the Fiddleback area between Douglas and Gillette, Wyoming. This includes the Cheyenne River Valley and Red and Rochelle Hills, which are havens for eagles, raptors, deer, elk, and antelope. The Upton-Osage area of the grassland, in the far northeast of Wyoming between Gillette and Newcastle, forms the foothills of the Black Hills. The terrain is low-sage and grass plains and thick pine-covered hills. Several reservoirs are stocked with small-mouthed bass and trout for year-round fishing. Some nineteen miles of trails wind through the hills and plains for hikers and bikers. A satellite unit, about two hours away from the district ranger station at Douglas, Wyoming, is the Spring Creek area, a prairie grass regime north of Gillette and extending to the Montana border.[40]

There are no developed campgrounds on the grassland, but there are picnic areas in the Spring Creek unit with toilets. An off-highway vehicle area in the Upton-Osage area near Gillette is frequently used, with many well-maintained roads because of the mining and drilling activity, according to Sprentall. Elevations range from 4,000 feet on the prairies to a high of 5,200 feet on the Rochelle Hills.

Wildlife on the grassland includes more than two hundred bird species, seventy-two observed mammals, thirty-eight wildflowers, and twelve common grasses. There are elk, pronghorn, deer, mountain lions and bobcats, coyotes, and three fox species including the endangered swift fox. Black-footed ferrets are to be reintroduced. There is active cattle grazing on the grassland and land exchange projects totaling fifty-five thousand acres are being pursued.

The Douglas Ranger Station administers Thunder Basin and the Laramie Peak unit of the Medicine Bow and Routt National Forests, with an annual budget of about $1.8 million and some forty permanent employees. Because of the huge mineral impact on the grassland, the staff includes geologists and other mineral program specialists, two archaeologists who also help prepare environmental impact statements for mining and drilling permits, a land purchase expert, and wildlife biologists and rangeland conservation specialists, according to Sprentall. He said that with the wide dispersal of public lands plus the intermingled private lands, there are about two million acres worked by his ranger station.

Southern Great Plains Grasslands

Five Southern Great Plains states, Kansas, Colorado, Oklahoma, New Mexico, and Texas, contain nine national grasslands in the Southern Great Plains, including the smallest ones in size and two that cross state lines. The Santa Fe Trail figures in three of the grasslands and the Cimarron NG is the most concentrated of all twenty grasslands, with few dispersed land units. The smallest grassland, McClellan Creek NG, at 1,449 acres, is primarily a recreation area surrounding Lake McClellan in Texas. Comanche NG in Colorado is the fourth largest and has views of the Rockies' Front Range along with a highly diversified terrain. Oil and gas are found on some of these grasslands. Much of the grasslands area is in the High Plains of the Great Plains, extending from Texas to the Pine Ridge Escarpment in western Nebraska. General terrain characteristics are prairie parkland, plains dry steppe, southwest plateau, and shrub province.

Pawnee National Grassland

Mountain plovers have made the Pawnee NG, 193,060 acres in northeast Colorado, a popular destination for amateur naturalists, professional biologists, and windshield tourists taking a thirty-six-mile birding tour. The grassland was once a stronghold for the plovers, now a declining species, and a "pretty good percentage" of the total number of plovers in the United States in the 1960s was found there, according to Beth Humphrey, wildlife biologist. Though their numbers are down now, the plovers are seen throughout the grassland and on adjoining private, cultivated land where the birds nest on bare ground or in very short grass. People come from Germany, the United Kingdom, and "all over the world" to view the birds, Humphrey said.

Pawnee is well known as a birder's paradise, with an observed bird count of 301 species, one of the highest of the grasslands. The bird tour is designed for cars and bikers and goes through the west and east portions of the sixty-mile-wide grassland, ending in the center at the Pawnee Buttes. These prominent landmarks are two buttes, 530 and 370 feet long and about 300 feet high, formed as the result of the erosion of uplifted sedimentary beds deposited by ancient seas. The butte cliff sides are popular nesting sites for raptors and swallows and the area is subject to closure from May 1 to June 31, when public access is prohibited. Other birds often seen along the tour are horned larks, lark buntings, eagles and hawks, including Swainson's hawks and northern harriers, burrowing owls in prairie dog towns, McCown's longspur, and chestnut-collared longspur.[41]

The grassland is widely dispersed with private land, though more blocked

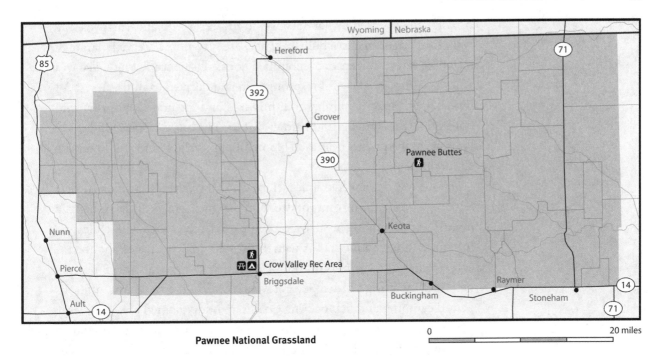

Pawnee National Grassland

off into contiguous areas on the west side. There is a ten-mile separation between the east and west units with private and state school lands, where cattle grazing dominates as a single land use. The grassland is managed for multiple uses of recreation, oil and gas production, wildlife and riparian protection, and cattle grazing. There are two grazing associations with 111 allotments and permits for eight thousand to nine thousand head of cattle. By mid-2004 several years of drought had reduced the cattle numbers and grazing time. Water is primarily supplied by windmills and stock tanks, with some plastic pipelines to carry water to pastures, according to Randy Reichert, range conservation specialist. There is not a large weed problem on the grassland, he noted, with just small patches of leafy spurge, knapweed, and Canadian thistle. "We are watching for salt cedar also," he said. The noxious weeds are controlled by chopping and manual spraying, or by cattle grazing.[42] Short grasses such as buffalo and blue grama dominate about 70 percent of the prairie on the grassland, with western and crested wheatgrass also present.

Flat to gently rolling plains dominate the grassland landscape, but are "occasionally bisected by habitats of mid-grasses, scrublands, arroyos, and cliff areas," according to a bulletin. There are fifty-nine observed mammals, including rare occurrences of mountain lions, plus bobcats, long-tailed weasels, the endangered swift fox, pronghorn and deer, elk, and the desert cottontail. Plant species number four hundred and include early spring wildflowers like the sand lily and Nuttall's violet. The biggest prairie show is in June, when the prickly pear cacti bloom in pink, yellow, and red flowers for about one week.[43]

There is one developed public facility, the Crow Valley Recreation Area, in a grove of elm and cottonwood trees on the open prairie. It has a ball diamond, group camping area, five camping pads, picnic area with tables and fire rings, water, and toilets. A winter off-road-vehicle area of about 1,200 acres, called The Main, is on the west unit, in the north-central portion near the Wyoming border. Several reservoirs, on the west unit, offer dispersed camping and fishing. The Coal is an oddly named area with steep banks popular for target shooting, including old TVs, computers, and appliances dragged in, illegally. Two law enforcement officers have been added to the eleven-person staff at the district ranger station in Greeley, Colorado, to control dumping and to patrol the large grassland area, according to Humphrey.

In the early Texas cattle-drive days following the Civil War, the Pawnee Buttes were well-known landmarks on the Goodnight-Loving Cattle Trail from Camp Concho, Texas.

Comanche National Grassland

Fossilized dinosaur tracks, Indian rock art, wild and scenic canyonlands, plus a nine-thousand-acre habitat for lesser prairie chickens bring visitors to Comanche NG in extreme southeast Colorado. At 443,438 acres, the grassland is the fourth largest and is in two units: Timpas, the northern, compact unit is administered by a ranger station at La Junta, Colorado; and Carrizo, the southern unit along the Oklahoma border, is more dispersed with checkerboard private lands and a ranger station at Springfield, Colorado.

Jurassic-era dinosaur tracks are on a flat sandstone slab on the banks of the Purgatoire River. At about 130 million years old, they are the result of allosaurus and brontosaurs strolling along the muddy bank of an ancient shallow lake. More than 1,300 tracks, including those of young brontosaurs, are visible along some one hundred trackways in a quarter-mile area, the largest track site in North America. The tracks have given insight into the social life of the animals.

The rock art is found throughout the grassland, but especially in Picket Wire Canyonlands, with petroglyphs, or incised carvings, and pictographs, or painted art. The U.S. Army transferred the sixteen-thousand-acre Picket

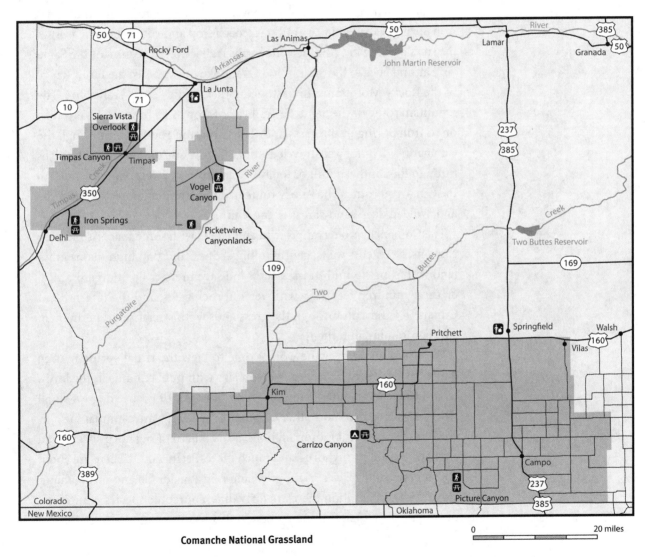

Comanche National Grassland

Wire lands to the grassland on December 3, 1991, after congressional action. Comanche Indians lived in the area from 1749 to 1805, but the rock art is much older and has unknown origins. Vogel, Carrizo, Timpas, and Picture Canyons have marked trails for the rock art and wildlife, and viewing is especially good at the Vogel site. There is a natural arch near Picture Canyon, with an arch rock trail.

Some forty noncontiguous miles of the old Santa Fe Trail can be seen in the grassland, on both north and south units, according to Tom Peters, district ranger. There is a half-mile loop walk on Timpas Creek with Trail views. Iron Spring was a Santa Fe Trail stagecoach stop and ruts are visible west of the site's parking lot. Another three-mile trail follows a section of the Santa Fe Trail and goes to the Sierra Vista Overlook with views of the Front Range of the Rocky Mountains. Limestone markers indicate the Trail route. The mountain route of the Santa Fe Trail went through La Junta and continued on to Iron Spring in the grassland. The Cimarron route went through the Cimarron NG, but a well-traveled Aubry Cutoff was pioneered in the 1850s through the southern unit of today's Comanche NG, west of and parallel to the Cimarron route. The Aubry route had more abundant water and grass and avoided deep sandy areas to the south.

The Comanche NG terrain is wild and scenic with some inaccessible deep canyons, steep cliff walls, gently rolling slopes, and flat, high plains grassland with short to mid-grasses and sand sage prairie. The Purgatoire River, three hundred feet deep with vertical rock walls, and the intermittent Cimarron River run through the grasslands, with streams and permanent springs draining into them.

Visitors from all over the world come to view the ritual spring mating dances of the lesser prairie chicken on leks with public blinds in the bird's largest Colorado habitat. Some six thousand acres of prairie dog towns all have burrowing owls and other compatible species. Native animals also include black bears and mountain lions, a small herd of big horn sheep, road runners, "lots of pronghorn," and much more, Peters said.[44] There are about 275 observed bird species, as the grassland is in a major fall and spring migratory fly way. In addition there are forty different reptile species, nine kinds of amphibian, eleven fish species, and sixty observed mammal species.

There is a good mixture of tree species, according to wildlife biologist Dave Augustine, including western juniper, pinion and ponderosa pine, and cottonwood and green ash along the river and stream bottomlands. Noxious weeds have invaded the grassland, including salt cedar along riparian woodlands, which are "knocking out the cottonwoods." The invader is controlled with herbicide and a mechanical hydroaxe, a front-end loader mounted with a slicing bar that cuts through the shrubs.

Five years of severe drought, from 1999 to mid-2004, along with strong evaporation rates of rainfall, has affected grassland cattle grazing, with a 25 percent reduction. Four grazing associations have 196 allotments for ninety-eight thousand permitted AUMs, or roughly ten thousand head of cattle, Augustine said. About 20 percent of the grassland has oil and gas leases, with seventeen producing wells and seventeen injection or disposal wells in the Campo oilfield.

The grassland has many Indian archaeological sites, before and after Euro-American settlement, and many homestead ruins along with stagecoach stops. The Delores Mission and Cemetery shows pioneer Mexican settlement, from 1871 to 1889. The Metcalf Ranch was the site of a stagecoach stop, from 1869 to 1871. There are no developed campgrounds on the grassland, but there are several picnic sites. None of the public sites have potable water and garbage should be carried out.

Comanche NG is wild and isolated, Augustine said, but with more than one hundred miles of trails, it is ideal for hiking, biking, horseback riding, hunting, and dispersed, primitive camping.[45]

Cimarron National Grassland

The Santa Fe Trail with its remarkable landmark, Point of Rocks, and the long riparian corridor of the mostly dry Cimarron River are outstanding features of the 108,175-acre Cimarron NG of southwest Kansas, administered by the Elkhart, Kansas, Ranger District office. The grassland is just east of the Comanche NG and borders Oklahoma.

The Cimarron route of the Santa Fe Trail winds for twenty-six miles through the grassland, and a modern nineteen-mile companion trail parallels it. Point of Rocks is a tall hill, third highest elevation in Kansas at 3,600

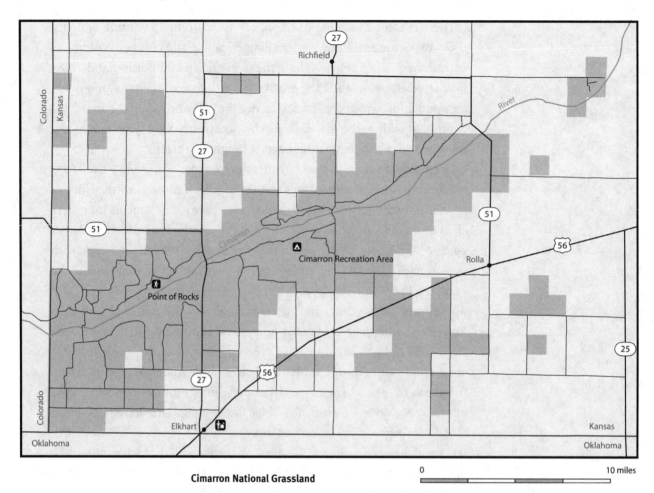

Cimarron National Grassland

0   10 miles

feet, and was a familiar landmark. It is near Middle Spring, an important, dependable water source on the Trail, and deep ruts can still be seen on short interpretive trails at both sites.

The Cimarron NG is one of the most compact of all twenty grasslands. Wildlife biologist Andy Chappell said there was a unique land buyer for the federal government in the 1930s who had a vision to consolidate the land as much as possible.[46]

The Cimarron River bisects the grassland and provides an important riparian corridor, with cottonwood and willows along the river bottom and woody draws leading to the uplands. The northern bank has tight loamy

23. Black Kettle Lake
is illuminated by
summer moonlight.

24. McClellan Creek National Grassland, Texas

soil with steep banks and broken land, while the south bank is sandy with silt loams and rolling sand hills leading to gently rolling prairie tableland. Wind erosion has been particularly severe here. There are about two hundred stock ponds and tanks fed with water from waterwheels, submerged pumps, and windmills. Forage grasses on the prairie are sand love, little and big bluestem, buffalo grass, and sideoats grama. Canadian thistle, bindweed, and Johnson grass are all problem weeds, but the biggest concern is salt cedar, a woody shrub, according to Nancy Brewer, rangeland management specialist. She said, "We have cut it, burned it, and sprayed it, but we're not getting rid of it."[47]

The animal and bird population is about the same as at Comanche NG, but there is a small elk herd that travels across the Kansas, Oklahoma, and Colorado borders. Scaled quail and lesser prairie chickens are common, and there are two leks with public blinds for the prairie chicken spring-booming rites. Elk and pronghorn were reintroduced to the grassland in the 1980s. A few swift-fox dens have been observed.

The Cimarron Recreation Area on the grassland has fourteen camping pads with tables and grills, potable water, toilets, stocked fishing ponds, and hiking trails. Primitive dispersed camping is allowed throughout the grassland except at the Cottonwood and Middle Spring picnic areas. The Turkey Trail along the river corridor has two trailheads, Conestoga and Murphy. Four-wheel-drive motorized vehicles are allowed.

Cattle grazing permits are administered through a grazing association, with some 3,500 head of cattle permitted annually. Reseeding of the badly eroded prairie was done in the 1940s and later, with sideoats grama, blue grama, sand love grass, crested wheatgrass, little bluestem and Canadian rye. Oil and gas production is important on the grassland.

Rita Blanca National Grassland

The central portion of the 92,989-acre Rita Blanca NG is a block of land with only one section of private land, and that feature is attracting a new kind of visitor, according to Nancy Walls, district ranger for both the Rita Blanca and Kiowa NGS. "People are coming to this large block of grassland just for the solitude and serenity of it," she said. "They want to experience

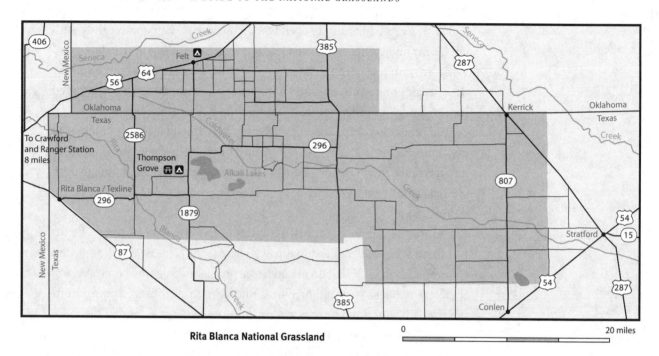

Rita Blanca National Grassland

0   20 miles

what it was like in the old days." The visit may be just for a day or with overnight camping, but the attraction is to be alone in the middle of a large expanse of native prairie without the trappings of modern development. That
kind of visit works on the grassland because there are less than three thousand head of cattle grazing there and the gently rolling prairie is normally
empty of people.

On the other hand, there is abundant wildlife on the grassland, with hundreds of bird species and large mammals such as mule and whitetail deer,
pronghorn, coyotes, fox, plus large prairie dog towns. Swift-fox dens have
been observed and research teams from Texas Tech University are studying
the animals. Scaled quail and pheasants provide good hunting, along with
deer and pronghorn. There are lots of raptors, according to Walls, along
with many species of shortgrass prairie birds such as grasshopper sparrows
and mountain plovers.[48]

Rita Blanca crosses state boundaries, with the largest portion in the Texas
Panhandle plus scattered blocks in the Oklahoma Panhandle. The district
ranger station is at Clayton, New Mexico. The Kerrick oil and gas field is

in the east Texas portion, but there are no drilling or operating wells now. The terrain is shortgrass prairie on the west portion and mixed prairie with mid- and short grasses on the east. The scattered units in Oklahoma and on the east Texas portion of the grassland are important as wildlife habitat islands among larger areas of cultivated land, Walls said.

An important grassland feature for birds are the numerous playa lakes that dot the landscape. Ranging from several hundred acres to ten to twenty acres in size, these are natural depressions on the plains with clay-sealed basins that collect rainfall and stay wet for months and years. According to Walls, they are closed systems that dry up in droughts, such as the severe three-year dry spell from 2001 to mid-2004, but can provide important riparian habitat in wet seasons, especially for migratory waterfowl. The lakes' origins are uncertain, as there was no glacial activity this far south to scoop out the depressions. They depend only on precipitation, not inflowing streams, for water. They also become an intermittent water source for congregating wildlife.

Other wetlands include a large alkali lake system with inflows from springs and intermittent streams, on private land but enclosed on three sides by the grassland. There are hundreds of stock ponds and water wells that depend in part on the Ogallala Aquifer underlying much of the Great Plains, along with windmills or solar or electric pumps.

Public facilities include the Thompson Grove Campsite in Texas with camping pads, picnic tables and grills, and restrooms but no potable water. The Felt Picnic Ground in Oklahoma has a site for group camping. An auto tour plan is being prepared for the Texas portion of the grassland.

There is no cattle grazing association for the Rita Blanca Grassland, so instead grazing permits go to individual ranchers, with thirty-two thousand AUMs allotted annually. However, stocking was down 30 to 60 percent during the three-year drought, to mid-2004, Walls said.

Kiowa National Grassland

The Canadian River winds through thirteen miles of the west portion of the widely separated Kiowa NG in New Mexico, with a beautiful nine-hundred-foot-deep canyon that is habitat for black bears, bobcats and wildcats, deer,

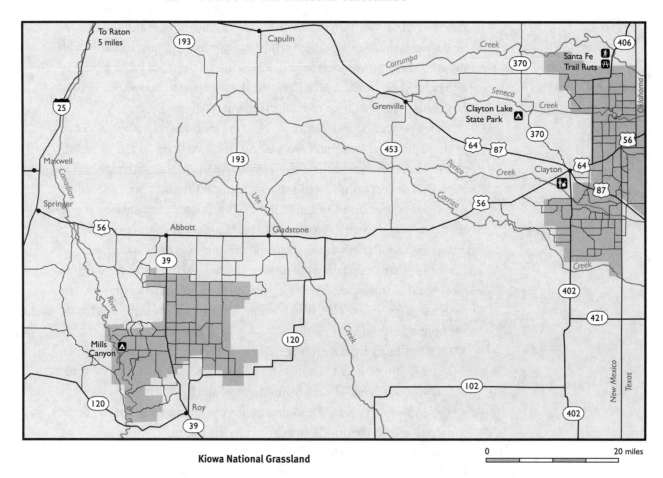

Kiowa National Grassland

0   20 miles

turkeys, and mountain lions. Barbary sheep, an African species, were introduced in 1985 and thrive there. Catfish can be caught and primitive camping is possible, with entry to the canyon on a dirt track only by four-wheel-drive vehicles with high axles. The red rock canyon is often inaccessible in the winter. A diverse tree canopy includes pinion and ponderosa pine (on the canyon rim), cottonwoods, willows, juniper, and oaks. There are woody draws with permanent and intermittent streams flowing into the river.

The grassland is in two widely separated units, the east one bumping the Texas border and the west unit some eighty-five miles west. Range conservationist Darrell Musick said that Kiowa and Rita Blanca NGs were combined under one ranger district at Clayton, New Mexico in 1994. "It is the most complicated" of all grassland administrations, he said, as they work in three states and six counties and deal with three state game-and-fish departments and three federal wildlife offices.[49] The district office now has twelve staff members, including a fire engine crew, according to Nancy Walls, district ranger.

The Kiowa NG has a three-mile portion of the Cimarron route of the Santa Fe Trail, with a new interpretive site that includes toilets and picnic tables and a marked trail for hiking and to view Trail ruts. The Trail lies between two resting and watering spots, McNees Crossing and Turkey Creek, with views of Rabbit Ears Mountain and Round Mound to the west. There are no other public facilities or campgrounds. There are no current operating oil and gas leases on the Kiowa.

Besides the Canadian River, the grassland also has playa lakes and stock ponds, like the Rita Blanca, with similar wildlife and bird species, besides those found in the canyonlands. Some of the forage grasses on Kiowa include sideoats, bluestem, silver bluestem, and galleta, with three-awned grass and sand dropseed in the lower succession stage, according to Musick. In the tighter clay soils the grasses include buffalo grass, Apache plume, sand sage, and skunkbush sumac, with little browse value, and small patches of salt brush, an alkali plant. The grassland terrain is juniper woodland on the west unit, interfacing to the east into shortgrass prairie.

There are 168 paid grazing leases for the Kiowa Grassland with a wide variety of grazing intensity on units that range from a single pasture up to fifty-three pastures. There are forty thousand AUMs allotted annually, for about three thousand head of cattle when fully stocked.

Black Kettle National Grassland

Shinnery oak shrubs and a great amount of water attract 45 general types of birds and 277 individual species to the 31,359-acre Black Kettle NG in western Oklahoma and the Texas Panhandle. Four developed manmade lakes, hundreds of stock ponds, springs, perennial and intermittent streams, and the Washita River make this the wettest of all grasslands, with water covering 10 percent of the area.

The Oklahoma portion of Black Kettle has widely scattered parcels with the Washita River running through the most concentrated part. There is a 576-acre unit surrounding Lake Marvin in Texas, close to the Canadian River and Lake Kiowa. The district ranger station is at Cheyenne, Oklahoma, with a staff of eight fulltime employees plus seasonal help. The developed Oklahoma lakes are Skipout Lake, Spring Creek Lake, and Black Kettle Recreation Area at Dead Indian Lake. These have camping with picnic tables, boat ramps, toilets, and water. Smaller lakes and ponds dot the countryside on both public and private land. Marvin Lake in Texas has a community center with a kitchen, six camping pads with electric hookups, picnic tables and toilets, boat ramp, and water. No hunting is allowed at Marvin Lake or the recreation areas of the Oklahoma lakes, according to natural resources specialist Tom Smeltzer.[50]

The combination of shrub and grass prairie—ranging from tall to short grasses—plus the abundant water attract huge numbers of birds, especially in migratory months, according to Chuck Milner, rangeland management specialist. The area is nationally known as hunting grounds for dove, bobwhite quail, deer, and Rio Grande turkeys. One bird count recorded eighty Mississippi kites congregated in a single area. River bottomlands attract bobcats and mountain lions or cougars, plus many beaver colonies. The lakes are popular fishing sites for catfish, black bass, saugeye, and pan fish. Milner noted that the grassland is a natural north-south, east-west crossroads for many species, and the Texas high plains and red bed plains meet in the grassland. "This is just a beautiful place," Milner said.

While there are sixty individual grazing permit holders, with allotments of twelve thousand AUMs annually or fifteen hundred to two thousand head of cattle, the land is also managed to encourage ground nesting birds. Prescribed fires burn four thousand to five thousand acres per year, topping off the shrubs, burning out the invasive eastern red cedar trees, and stimulating forage grasses such as big and little bluestem, sideoats grama, blue grama, Indian grass, and switch grass. Scotch thistle is a major noxious plant and is controlled with some spraying and digging out by hand. There are twenty-one producing gas wells on the Black Kettle Oklahoma unit with one to two new wells drilled annually; many older wells have been plugged and the land reclaimed. Underground pipelines intersect the grassland.

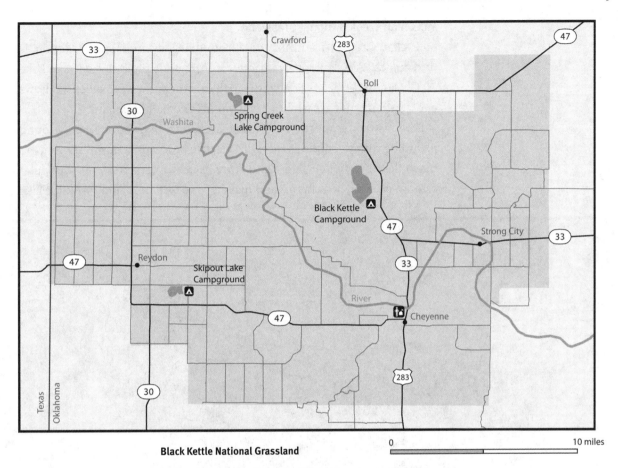

Black Kettle National Grassland

0   10 miles

The rare shinnery oak community is one of the fastest shrinking ecosystems in the nation, according to Milner. The shrubs feature several subspecies and grow two to five feet high in circular mini-plantations, or motts, which range from twenty to fifty feet in diameter. The grassland is shrub and grass dominated, plus river bottomlands with woody draws and tall to mid-grasses on rolling hills. There is "a lot of urban interface and cultivated fields" near the grassland, Milner said.[51] A network of paved highways and gravel roads means most areas of the grassland are less than a mile from a road. The grassland was named after a Southern Cheyenne Indian chief who was killed along with his entire village at the Washita Massacre, by troops led by George Custer in 1868.

McClellan Creek National Grassland

McClellan Creek NG, administered from the Cheyenne Ranger Station, is the smallest grassland at 1,449 acres. It surrounds the hundred-acre Lake McClellan in the Texas Panhandle with canyonlands, wooded creek draws, and grassy upland areas, about half woods and half grassland.

The grassland is mostly a recreation area, with an elaborate campground including thirty camping pads with electric hookups, a dump station, picnic tables and shelters, a general store, toilets, and water. It is a popular fishing site, with boat ramps and marshes and wetlands along with the lake.

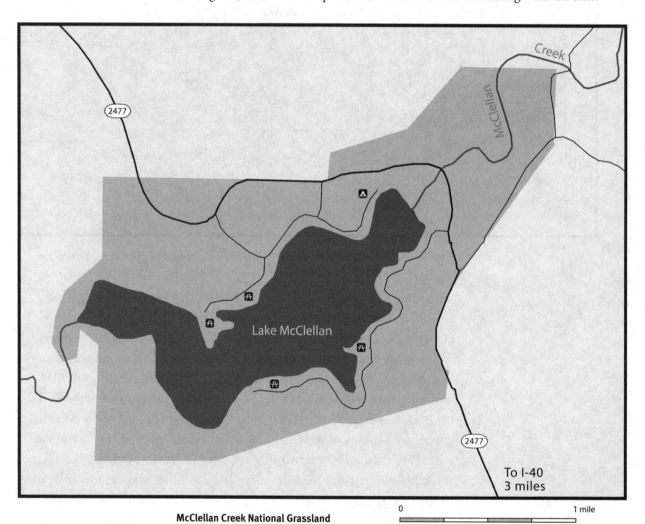

McClellan Creek National Grassland

0   1 mile

There are fifteen old oil wells still producing after thirty years, but no new drilling. No hunting is allowed on the grassland. There is an eight-mile off-road-vehicle trail, plus extensive paved roads.

Caddo National Grassland

More than six million Texans in the Dallas–Fort Worth metroplex live within driving range of the Caddo and Lyndon B. Johnson National Grasslands. They have lakes with developed campgrounds and open public land that is rare in Texas, attracting many thousands of visitors year-round. Jim Crooks, district ranger for both grasslands, said public use for them has doubled between 2000 and 2004. "They are probably the most used of any of the grasslands," he said. Their ranger district station is at Decatur with a work center at Caddo.[52]

Caddo NG, 17,873 acres, is separated into three units in northeast Texas, near the Oklahoma border, and north of Dallas. The biggest unit, Bois d'Arc, surrounds Coffee Mill Lake and two arms of Lake Davy Crockett. A smaller unit surrounds Fannin Lake along the Red River. The more distant Ladonia unit is unusual open prairie in checkerboard blocks. There are twelve camping units on the 450-acre West Lake Davy Crockett, with picnic facilities, water, and restrooms. East Lake Davy Crockett, also 450 acres, has picnic units, restrooms, and a concrete boat ramp. The larger, 750-acre Coffee Mill Lake, has a fishing pier and ramp, picnic units, and drinking water, while the smaller 75-acre Fannin Lake has only a primitive boat ramp. A Bois d'Arc trailhead includes twelve campsites, toilets and water, and a multi-use trail used especially for horseback riding. There are twenty miles of trails on the grassland.

A former Civilian Conservation Corps camp built by the Resettlement Administration in 1936 occupies one hundred acres on a bluff at the Fannin unit and is on the National Register of Historic Places. After long neglect, eight cabins, a lodge, caretaker's house, and bathhouse are being restored, as private donations and public funds allow. In 2004, some forty-five to fifty people from throughout the nation, working as Passport in Time volunteers, lived for two weeks at the twenty-acre compound to help restore the historic buildings.

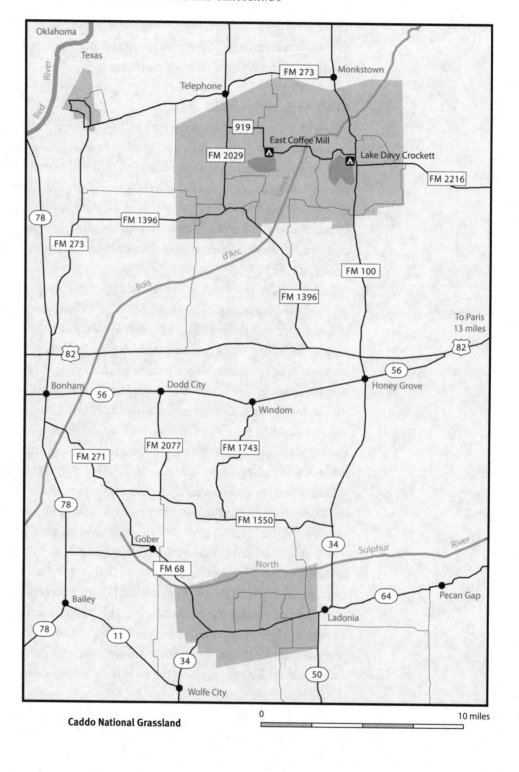

Caddo National Grassland

0   10 miles

The grassland's Ladonia unit has a rare ecosystem of black land prairie. It is a "shrink-swell" soil type of unusual moving gumbo with a clay base. The soil swells when wet and stays wetter, but when dry it shrinks back and splits. This causes houses to move and foundations to crack, Crooks said. Tall grasses on the prairie include Indian grass and little and big bluestem. Wildlife includes typical prairie species such as deer, turkey, and quail.

Lyndon B. Johnson National Grassland

An astounding one thousand plant species have been observed on the 20,309-acre LBJ (formerly Cross Timbers) NG, thirty-five miles north of Fort Worth, according to Jim Crooks, district ranger. Spread out shotgun fashion in a triangular area, with a few satellite blocks, the unit is partly rolling, open, grand prairie, and post and blackjack oak savannah. It also includes elm and eastern red cedar trees. It is in the Texas crossroads of eastern timber and open grassland. The plants include a profusion of wildflowers in the spring, bringing many visitors. They also attract an observed eighty-eight different butterfly species, including the general types of swallowtails, whites and sulphurs, brush-footed butterflies, and skippers.[53] A bird checklist shows 228 species including rare sightings of whooping crane, long-eared owl, greater scaup duck, red-necked phalarope sandpiper, Townsend's solitaire thrush, western bluebird, and Henslow's sparrow.[54]

People are attracted to the grassland's lakes with excellent public facilities. The thirty-five-acre Black Creek Lake has fourteen campsites, boat ramp and fishing bridge, and toilets. On the eighteen-acre Clear Lake there is a fishing pier, primitive boat ramp, and picnic area. Only canoes are allowed on Windmill Lake, a small fourteen-acre body, featuring fly-fishing. The forty-acre Cottonwood Lake has a concrete boat ramp and trailhead for a four-mile hiking trail to Black Creek Lake. In all, LBJ has fifty miles of multi-use trails. Other facilities include Tadra Point with parking, camping, and horse facilities; Red Deer archery unit with seven targets and picnic tables; and Valley View, a designated bird-dog training area with fifteen camping units, pavilion, restroom, and water for horses.

Horseback riding is a major attraction to the two grasslands, as well as star gazing, hiking and biking, geocache treasure hunts, hunting and fishing,

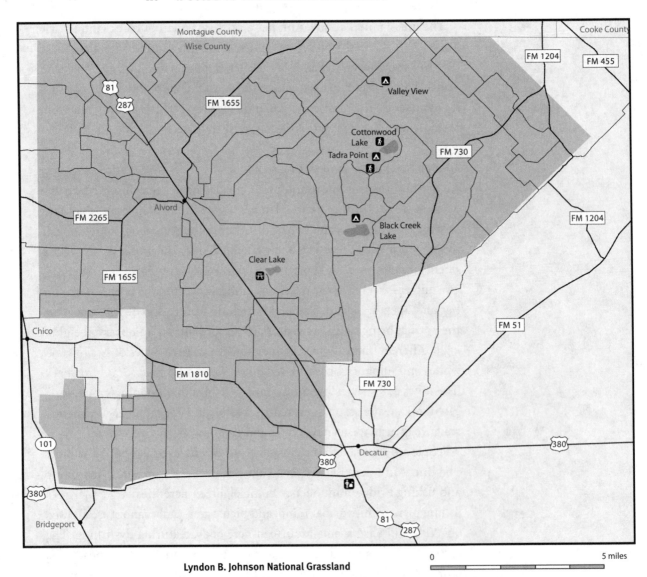

Lyndon B. Johnson National Grassland

picnics, photography, camping, flower-, butterfly-, and bird-watching, and just plain serenity sessions on open, public land, Crooks said. LBJ wildlife include many fish species such as largemouth bass, perch, and blue, channel, and yellow catfish. The list also includes whitetail deer, coyote, bobcat, red fox, wild turkey, quail, and many small mammals in a diverse habitat. There are few problems of noxious weeds or invasive plant species, Crooks said, in the tallgrass prairie. On both grasslands, Caddo and LBJ, there are thirty-five grazing permits for about twelve hundred head of cattle. The grasslands are divided into management areas for grazing and wildlife emphasis under a ten-year plan, but, Crooks said, "we manage for wildlife throughout them." The two grasslands are about 130 miles apart. There is a large natural gas formation underlying the LBJ Grassland, with ninety active oil and gas wells and more being drilled every year. An underground pipeline system to a nearby refinery intersects the grassland. About $170,000 a year goes to Wise County from grassland mineral royalties, divided between schools and roads.

Grasslands National Park of Canada

Bison are getting a large, fenced home of seventy sections (44,800 acres) on the Grasslands National Park of Canada, in southwest Saskatchewan along the United States border with Montana. Fifty yearling calves will be in place by summer 2005, according to wildlife biologist Pat Fargey, to be winter-fed in pens then let out to roam on spring and summer grass.[55] After four to five years, the growing herd will be culled with pasture kills and butchering, leaving the carcasses on the prairie, in the Indian tradition. The bison are part of a long-term management plan approved by Parliament in May 2003. Plans are being made to introduce cattle, probably through a fee system with ranchers, using intensive grazing over short times.

The park is part of the Canadian Protected Heritage System, protecting examples of thirty-nine natural regions, and it represents the prairie grasslands. It was born in 1988 after an initial dispute between the provincial and federal governments over mineral rights in 1981. Since then all mineral leases have been extinguished and there are no oil or gas wells on the park, although there are natural gas wells within five miles of the boundary, Fargey said. The park will enclose 900 square kilometers (350 square miles) in two separate blocks when fully developed, and is currently 478 square kilometers (185 square miles).

The Frenchman River Valley, a glacial meltwater channel with deeply dissected plateaus, coulees, and a seventy-mile butte, dominates the park's west block. There are bare white salt flats left behind by ancient oceans, hardpan soil with few plants, although the miniature red samphire survives there. Rock Creek flows through the east block with the Killdeer Badlands extending to the prairie and Wood Mountain uplands. The prairie plants include mid- and short grasses such as blue grama and needle and thread, plus prickly pear cactus and gumbo evening primrose.

More than three hundred native animals have been observed on the park, including one hundred and ninety bird species and fifteen endangered, threatened, or special-concern species, Fargey said. The Canadian list of endangered species found at the park includes the mountain plover, sage thrasher, burrowing owl, greater sage grouse, and swift fox. The latter was reintroduced in the early 1990s and the population has expanded into Montana. Threatened species are the loggerhead shrike and Sprague's pipit, and the newest on the list, the Mormon metal mark butterfly. Of special concern are the short-eared owl, eastern shorthorn lizard, eastern yellow-bellied racer, long-billed curlew, ferruginous hawk, northern leopard frog, and the black-tailed prairie dog. Prairie dog colonies on and around the park are their northernmost habitat in North America and the only ones in Canada. Other wildlife includes animals found throughout the U.S. national grasslands, such as deer, pronghorn, bobcats and an occasional mountain lion, coyotes, badgers, skunks, rabbits, prairie rattlesnake, and mink.

The park's visitor center is at Val Marie on the west block, open daily in spring and summer and on weekdays otherwise. Mankota, the nearest town for the east block, also has restaurants, fuel, campgrounds, and accommodations. A favorite park activity is horseback riding, and two outfitters provide horses and camping trips. There are daily guided hikes from the visitor center in July and August, using some of the eight hiking trails in the park. The Wood Mountain Regional Park adjoins the grassland park, with a campground with electric hookups, swimming pool, laundry and shower, concession booth, picnic area, and the Rodeo Ranch Museum. Primitive tent camping is encouraged anywhere in the park and there is limited room for self-contained recreational vehicles at two former ranch sites. There is no potable water in the park. A Frenchman River auto eco-tour takes about

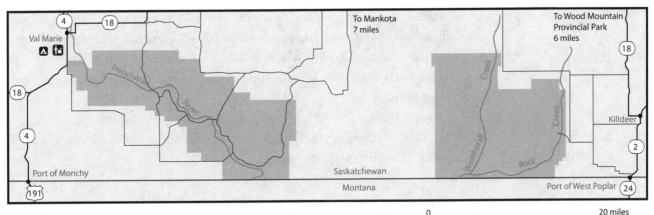

Grasslands National Park of Canada

0   20 miles

two and a half hours, with brochure and auto cassette at the visitor center.

Sitting Bull, a famous Sioux Indian chief, brought his followers to this area in 1876, after the Little Bighorn Battle with George Custer in Montana, before returning to the United States where he was eventually murdered.

A major characteristic of the U.S. national grasslands and the Grasslands National Park of Canada is their semiarid, gently rolling prairies with an ocean of grass. They are mostly checkerboard reserves, intermingled with private lands, often on a five-to-one ratio of private to public lands. But the federal land is also highly diversified and each grassland has unique features. They are a major resource for native flora and fauna and a refuge for hundreds of troubled species.

Although visitors can travel for days on the grasslands without seeing other people, the land is becoming more familiar for tourists, and homes slowly move closer and closer. Grasslands near larger population centers are becoming especially popular for a wide variety of outdoor activities.

Even though there is an increasing payout of mineral royalties from the grasslands, their budget for administration, recreation, public use infrastructure, and wildlife biodiversity has remained static. "The whole agency has had a flat budget the last couple years. It is holding its own, and that is good because other agencies have seen a decline," according to the acting head of the grasslands, Rick Caples.[56] Mineral income is about $70 million annually, while grasslands costs are around $20 million per year. It is difficult to separate out exact costs of grasslands mixed in with national forests, plus administrative and professional support from forest, regional and headquarters staff in Washington DC. Only money for fire plans has increased recently.

Changes are slowly making their way through the grassland structure, and they will be examined in the final chapter. As well, future alternatives for the national grasslands will be explored.

25. Great egrets in tree,
Caddo National Grassland

26. Garden coreopsis line the many back roads
of the Lyndon B. Johnson National Grassland.

III. BISON INSTEAD OF CATTLE?

I wanted more time to watch the buffalo, more time to understand what had changed the psyche of the herd. But my scent cone was rolling in the wind like a powder-blue fly line and so I gave up watching the herd and concentrated on the old cow that would feel it first.

I watched closely, feeling my scent straighten out with the shifted wind—the invisible fly line—and just when I would have lifted the rod up for a gentle presentation, the cow's head came up with a violent shake. She had been lying down but came up with fierce eyes and an odd grunt that set the herd into motion. Suddenly everyone was on their feet. There was a flurry of action over the entire hillside, and several cows actually started in my direction. Perhaps I should have been frightened but I was too amazed. My little herd of sweet, tame buffalo had become something quite different and I could not understand why. The bulls loped down the hill to meet the cows who had started up the draw. They were vacating the bowl at a run, old cows first and bulls at the back. I stood to watch them go, frustrated that my presence would make them react that way. But as the buffalo lined out for the top of the hill I saw that this frantic herd action should not be taken personally. It was basic instinct. As I watched the first three mature cows top the hill and disappear, I saw a puff of golden fuzz running at the flank of each.[1]

Those puffs of fuzz were the first bison calves born in a herd being developed by Dan O'Brien, South Dakota rancher and author. They represented a new way of life for him, and a restoration of an old life on the Great Plains. He is winter-grazing bison on twenty thousand acres of the Buffalo Gap NG along the Cheyenne River.

Seventy years have passed since administrators of President Franklin Roosevelt's New Deal revolution began buying land and laying out the organization to rehabilitate 11.3 million acres in America. The restoration has been mostly successful. On the national grasslands, recurrent droughts have hurt the range but not destroyed it. Thousands of stock ponds serve both cattle and wildlife. Riparian areas are better protected and management policies provide for public recreation, wildlife diversity, and threatened species protection. In many cases wildlife lives alongside disruptive mineral extraction, and pollution is minimized. Cattlemen have regulations for grazing and height standards of the grass are enforced to prevent overgrazing. In drought, ranchers often voluntarily cut the number of cattle and their time on public lands. Neighboring ranchers who learn by example have picked up good management policies from grasslands staff. Ranchers raise wildlife as well as livestock; many are proud of that and are protective of the animals. The soil and water conservation goals of the New Deal are largely met.

The social revolution expected by New Deal idealists did not flower, however. The way out of the terrible depression of the 1930s was through war mobilization and the drought's end, with new world markets for farm commodities. Subsistence communities and homesteads, rural resettlement, garden cities, and new farm villages alone did not end the Depression. They helped as relief in the immediate emergency, but became costly and unpopular with lawmakers as well as bureaucrats, and quietly slipped away in the new excitement of a nation at war. The country urbanized, farm efficiency exploded, and new problems now confront a rural sector that suffered so much in the Depression.

In the semiarid prairies of the West and the Great Plains where the national grasslands are located, deep rural areas are losing population—especially young people—and towns are dying. As the years have passed, the wisdom of the Buffalo Commons concept has been validated. That theory notes that 110 deep rural counties of the Great Plains—isolated, with low populations and scarce services—will continue to lose population, family income, and community infrastructure, and new uses for the land need to be found. Since Frank and Deborah Popper publicized it in 1987, the Buffalo Commons case has come to many of the nation's poorest counties that are located in the Great Plains. Each subsequent census since 1930 has recorded population losses, some severe, in deep rural counties. Main-street businesses are closing and some areas have recovered the frontier status of only two people, or fewer, per square mile. In ranch country, families sell out when the third or fourth generation after the Depression won't come back home. Fewer ranches with more cattle making less profit than in the past means less retail business for small towns. The big spike in cattle prices of 2003 and 2004 only reaffirms the boom-and-bust cycle of cattle. Earlier, in some years of the 1980s and 1990s, low cattle prices and drought often kept cattle income below the cost of production. In nearly all deep rural Great Plains counties, the biggest income maker is not agriculture and cattle but transfer payments from government sources, such as pensions and commodity subsidies. The older the population grows, the more that will be true.

In fact the wealth of these areas that surround the grasslands is mostly contained in land for cash-poor, land-rich residents. And that is another problem. A large portion of the income and wealth tied up in land could be exported, upon the death of owners, if heirs live out-of-state and don't plan to return. Without family takeovers of ranches, the land is consolidated under fewer owners, meaning fewer families, corporate-style ranching, and less support for local communities. The New Deal agricultural revolution was based on new ideas for submarginal land use. They worked and are working. People, however, have not necessarily benefited. It may be time to look at new alternatives to the current use of the national grasslands to help find those benefits. Here are three general alternatives for the future.

STAY THE COURSE The first and most likely alternative is to stay the course, a role the Forest Service is now generally following. Many of the recent Forest Service management plans that include national grasslands are completed or are being worked on, and there are few, if any, dramatic changes approved or foreseen. Change will be in small increments. In the recently completed Northern Great Plains Plan, two wilderness area designations were approved—the first ever for national grasslands—but there are no plans to submit them to Congress for action, according to Rick Caples, acting deputy chief of the national grasslands. He also said there is very little land for roadless area designations, although the Forest Service has initiated a proposal to restrict all travel in the grasslands to designated roads, as some regions already do. There is "strong interest" in getting off-highway vehicles restricted to designated areas, Caples said. There would still be open access to grasslands for hiking and biking and lots of open roads and trails, but "we want to eliminate cross-country [vehicle] travel," he said.[2] Another change in the new management plan is granting more acreage for reintroducing black-footed ferrets, including twenty-five thousand acres in the Fall River District of the Buffalo Gap NG, and in Thunder Basin NG.

There have been and will continue to be conflicts between the Forest Service and grazing permit holders over the number of cattle and length of grazing periods on the grasslands, especially when drought reduces grass production. This is particularly seen in actions dropping the AUM numbers per pasture and in the expected standards of leaving high structure grass when grazing. The Forest Service won a long and contentious administrative and legal battle over reducing AUMs at Fort Pierre NG (*Central South Dakota Grazing District v. U.S. Forest Service*), affirming that grazing is not a right, but a privilege. AUMs were dropped from 70,000 annually to 51,558 and the grazing district disputed this. Judge Arlen Beam of the U.S. Eighth Circuit

Court of Appeals on June 15, 2001, affirmed a federal district court decision favoring the Forest Service. Beam grew up in the Nebraska Sand Hills ranch country and worked as a cowhand.

The trend in cattle decline on national grasslands is confirmed in the annual head count. In 1976 there were 234,501 animals authorized for pasturage on the grasslands. That has dropped to 184,925 head permitted to graze in 2003, but the actual numbers of cattle on the grasslands that year were only 153,345 (compared to 96.1 million total head of cattle in America in 2003). Grazing fees on the grasslands totaled $1,667,789 in 1976, declining to $491,753 in the 2002–03 grazing year.

There will be a steady trend toward emphasizing more multiple-use resource management on grasslands. This will include more public use as populations reach closer and closer to certain grasslands and their open spaces become increasingly popular as a desired destination for many activities. Annual grazing on allotted pastures will be likely to decrease, allowing the grass to recover in one to three years. According to District Ranger Bill Perry, "What we need to do is to replicate the past and rest the pastures." Perry explained that, before Euro-American settlement, bison came and went on the plains and would not graze areas for two or three years.[3] This allowed vegetation to recover and provided increased nourishment for all types of native wildlife.

RETURN TO TRADITIONAL GRAZING Ranchers who hold grazing permits often disagree with these priorities, and they support a second, but unlikely, alternative future for the grasslands. They prefer a return to the traditional grazing on public lands of the 1940s and 1950s, before the grasslands were authorized. Since 1938, on L-U project lands under the Soil Conservation Service, grazing districts and associations were pretty much in charge of land management, and there were fewer government agents with smaller budgets. Thus there was little interference with grazing as the primary management objective. Local ranchers established conservation districts through votes and organized grazing associations for cooperative use of intermingled public and private land. They implemented conservation practices, with help from scs experts, and they made infrastructure improvements such as constructing fences, pipelines, stock dams and tanks, and windmills. They hired cowboys to repair fences, count cattle, and enforce grazing rules. These are continuing practices.

While grazing associations are still important in the Northern Great Plains and the West, there are fewer in Kansas, southeast Colorado, New Mexico, Oklahoma, and Texas, where permitees work individually with the Forest Service. Management plans have now widely changed grazing practices and bigger, more professional Forest Service staffs with larger budgets support the multi-use philosophy. Because they must make a profit, ranchers have more of a single-purpose philosophy.

Another major issue for ranchers is the spread of prairie dog towns and the reintroduction of species, such as black-footed ferrets, that rely on them. Ranchers most often view prairie dogs as rodent pests who ruin pastures and compete for the grass. The prairie dogs "are now coming on private, taxable land," and ruining the land, according to Nate Skjoldal, president of the Association of National Grasslands (ANG).[4] This group, formed in 1978, represents sixteen grazing associations in North and South Dakota, Wyoming, and Nebraska, and lobbies for their policies in Washington DC, with the Public Land Council. He said there should be buffer zones on the grasslands, separating prairie dog colonies from private lands. "We can poison the prairie dogs up to the [grassland] fence, but a year later they are back on our land. We need a good neighbor policy," Skjoldal said.

The ANG passed a resolution to support removing the national grasslands from the Forest Service. They prefer jurisdiction by the Bureau of Land Management, with easier grazing rules, or privatization of the lands. "We are a thorn in the side of the Forest Service," to insure that they don't have complete control, Skjoldal said. They see the Forest Service as "trying to promote wildlife emphasis more than commodity production." They maintain that their ranches provide economic vitality to local communities and their private lands provide important property taxes to counties. They are against roadless areas that block off existing roads and cut off access to their allotments, or new roadless areas that could eliminate future roads that may be needed.

Ranchers have important political clout; working with other cattlemen's groups, they lobby hard to keep Forest Service policies friendly to them, relying on nearly seven decades of relationships with government agencies. They have kept permit fees generally under two dollars an AUM in the West, far less than private grazing leasing rates, even after adding in costs from their grazing association. The fees are not likely to be raised.

However, ranchers face a steady erosion of grazing time, more public use of the land they lease—which is always open to the public—and less popular support for their role on the national grasslands. Their battle will be to keep current benefits, rather than make changes favorable to them.

CONSOLIDATION, BIODIVERSITY, AND TOURISM Ranchers would both win and lose in a third alternative future of blocking up the grasslands into compact units through purchases and land exchanges, creating more biodiversity, and attracting tourists to open wildlife reserves.

The big secret of the national grasslands is that Congress did not specifically approve livestock grazing on them. Only through administrative orders of the secretary of agriculture has a license been issued to continue grazing allotments and permits for fees. The grazing tradition is long and strong, but has no legislative basis. The basic law allowing the purchase of submarginal land for Land Utilization projects is the Bankhead-Jones Farm Tenant Act. It does not mention agriculture or grazing, but calls for the USDA

> to develop a program of land conservation and land utilization, including the retirement of lands which are submarginal or not primarily suitable for cultivation, in order thereby to correct maladjustments in land use, and thus assist in controlling soil erosion, reforestation, preserving natural resources, mitigating floods, preventing impairment of dams and reservoirs, conserving surface and subsurface moisture, protecting the watersheds of navigable streams, and protecting the public lands, health, safety, and welfare.[5]

The Taylor Grazing Act, which does approve livestock grazing on public lands, applies only to the U.S. Bureau of Reclamation and not the Forest Service. And the 1960 Multiple Use–Sustained Yield Act, which provides for grazing as one of the uses, applies only to the national forests and not the grasslands, according to the USDA Office of General Counsel.[6]

Agriculture on the grasslands, however, was reaffirmed in the secretary of agriculture's administrative order of June 23, 1960, which established the national grasslands. They "shall be administered for outdoor recreation, range, timber, watershed, and wildlife and fish purposes," the order stated. Further, they shall be managed "for multiple use and sustained yield" and to "maintain and improve soil and vegetative cover and to promote the development of grassland agriculture in the areas of which the national grasslands are a part." All "leases, permits, agreements, contracts, and memoranda of understanding" affecting the lands will continue in force.[7] Clearly there were to be multiple uses in grasslands management, and they were to serve as demonstration areas for excellent soil and water conservation practices and grazing techniques. Permits for grazing allotments would continue. Administrative orders can, of course, be revamped or negated without congressional action.

There is, thus, an inherent dichotomy built into national grasslands' management. The intent of the Bankhead-Jones Act was to remove people from submarginal lands and put those degraded lands to uses other than farming. As one analyst notes, "what is beyond dispute is that these lands were to be acquired, held, and managed for public benefit—and grazing is not a public benefit."[8] But there are nearly seven decades of history and tradition of private grazing on public lands that became the national grasslands. In fact, throughout the West, there are 262 million acres of public land grazed by domestic livestock. At the same time, the federal government in 2004 paid farmers $1.66 billion to take 34.7 million acres out of crop cultivation, under the Conservation Reserve Program. There were twelve million acres idled in five Northern Great Plains states alone. The Grasslands Reserve Program offers another $50 million to keep grasslands unplowed. The 3.8 million acres of national grasslands being managed for about $20 million a year is miniscule compared to those programs.

The multiple uses of national grasslands have a fatal flaw. National policy includes the single use of private livestock grazing. That means the national grasslands are cut up into pastures with internal fencing that discourages free roaming wildlife such as bison and other large mammals, and bottles up the open grassland space. Prairie dogs, a keystone grassland animal, are seen as competitors for grass by ranchers, who would eliminate them. Bison, on the other hand, are self sufficient on an open range, do not trample riparian areas, and need little care during winter months. Their biggest expense on the grasslands would be taller and heavier exterior fences to keep them from roaming outside the grassland boundaries.

Daniel Licht, a fish and wildlife biologist, wrote in 1997 that a congressional edict for "multiple use" plans on public lands "as currently defined and practiced is impossible," and it most often favors livestock grazing for profit.[9] In addition, the fragmentation of the grasslands into checkerboards of public and private lands works against many of the desired multiple uses, such as public recreation and wildlife diversity and production. While islands of public land, floating in more acres of private pastures or cropped fields, are managed for wildlife, they are not as effective as large open blocks of land where biodiversity has free rein. Licht summarizes:

> Grassland biodiversity conservation, as defined in the more comprehensive sense (genetic, taxonomic, and community processes), cannot be ensured on private lands. Only on very large tracts, the type typically associated with public ownership, can many of these species and processes continue unfettered . . . Society needs to accept the candid truth that if comprehensive grassland biodiversity protection is to occur, it will happen on large tracts of contiguous public lands.[10]

Consolidation of grasslands tracts has proceeded, but it is not a top priority of new management plans or Washington headquarters. It can occur in two ways, through land exchanges or purchases. For ranchers, land exchanges make the most sense, as it also consolidates their ranch operations, brings pastures closer to their headquarters, and eliminates pesky public use of their land. This is a win for both sides. Land purchases for consolidation are more difficult because there is little money available, there may not be willing sellers, and local officials are reluctant to see more land taken off tax rolls. Neither Congress nor USDA leaders have shown interest in land purchases.

However, if there is to be true multiple use of national grasslands, cattle grazing needs to be downplayed, lands need to be consolidated, and more funding is needed for wildlife management, public facilities, riparian protection, and recreational use. Keystone wildlife species, such as bison and prairie dogs, are essential to such plans, as they foster the environment for many allied species that depend upon them. True multiple-use plans also boost greater public interest in grasslands to enjoy the open spaces, view wildlife, and participate in outdoor activities. That brings tourists who may support local communities and retailers as much, or more so, than livestock production. There can be more businesses grown, like a renovated cow town bed-and-breakfast near the Oglala NG and a bison producer on the Buffalo Gap NG who sells meat nationwide through the Internet.

Where would the money come from for additional infrastructure funding, land trades and purchases, and wildlife production and research on national grasslands? The answer is from the grasslands themselves. Mineral royalties generate about $70 million per year. About half of that is returned to states and counties, leaving some $30 to $35 million in the U.S. Treasury. If Congress put just half of that amount, or $15 million, per year for ten years into a $150-million trust fund (yielding $7.5 million or more per year in interest) for the grasslands, there would be enough to carry out several important changes. District rangers could apply for funding with well-reasoned plans for land exchanges or purchases, for fostering wildlife diversity, or for needed public access improvements. Land exchanges through third parties, such as grazing associations, which can take five or more years to complete, could be financed out of the trust fund to relieve all parties of expensive land assessments, surveys, and title clearance. Many federal agencies can already apply for money to buy land, through the Land and Water Conservation Fund; there can also be a fund dedicated just for national grasslands.

There has already been a major study done to support such work. The Northern Plains Conservation Network in 2004 released Ocean of Grass, a conservation assessment for the Northern Great Plains. Sixteen private organizations sponsored the work, to "chart a future that integrates conservation with the renewal of the human communities and economy of the Northern Great Plains." The report notes that the "grand experiment" of agriculture that converted the oceans of grass to cattle and wheat "has had mixed results," as evidenced by declining towns, young people moving out, and failed local economies. Great Plains landscapes are so highly altered that the "functional role of several key species has been severely reduced or eliminated."[11]

The report identified ten core areas of two million acres or more, each in the Northern Great Plains and Canada, as suitable for large-scale conservation restoration as biodiversity reserves. Four of the core areas include national grasslands: Little Missouri, Thunder Basin, Buffalo Gap, and Oglala. The Thunder Basin–Oglala area is a prime candidate for such management and could join Buffalo Gap NG along with the Black Hills National Forest, Custer State Park, Badlands National Park, and Pine Ridge Indian Reservation lands as excellent models for combining large, open grasslands to restore native species, from bison to prairie dogs. There is already a huge tourist appeal in the Black Hills. Bison and prairie dogs, and related species, are already present and could be expanded. The area has the only successful black-footed ferret reintroduction, on the Wall unit of the Buffalo Gap NG.

Tyler Sutton, president of the Grassland Foundation, said the key issue in proposing such an ecosystem management plan for the grasslands is getting local community support. "We need people to support a planning process to protect biodiversity and create an economic opportunity for private land owners and community residents," he said. With different types of land ownership and use involved, they must be at least loosely coordinated, with management objectives for both public and private lands. The end result of such efforts would be to "create a land use regime of public and private land to bring back a full complement of native Great Plains species compatible with local economies. This is an economic opportunity for communities," he said, for tourism, hunting, tours, and many retail outlets. "But you need community support, you can't impose it." The key may be a local land trust to purchase lands, changing usage from cattle to native wildlife. "Until we accept as public policy changing the management, over time, of 10 to 15 percent of the land on the North American Great Plains from cattle to biodiversity, small towns will continue to wither and die," Sutton claimed.[12]

This community process for local support is slowly moving ahead in one town, Chadron, Nebraska. Butch Ellis, former Forest Service resources coordinator now with the Nature Conservancy in Chadron, said meetings have been held there about a land trust. "The people meeting together agreed there are lands with values other than agriculture," and that a land trust could look at improvement practices, conservation easements, and "on some occasions buy important parcels of land." He noted that the Sugarloaf Grazing Association of the Oglala NG would be perfect for the new kind of management as they have an office, secretary, and infrastructure to set up hunts and tours and to help with new tourism businesses. "But this would be new and different, and not traditional" to their methods, he said.[13]

Any such process on the Great Plains should include Native Americans. They have a large presence with big reservations and growing populations, and they already support a keystone species, bison. Fred DuBray, president of the Intertribal Bison Cooperative, said his group has fifty-three member tribes in eighteen states, with some fifteen thousand head of bison. Their primary purpose is to restore bison on tribal lands for their cultural relationship to tribal members. The cooperative owns two bison packing plants, in South Dakota and Montana, with capacity to process sixty head a day at each plant. "We are trying to restore these buffalo back as a wildlife resource. The relationship between tribe and buffalo means the buffalo must retain their own position as wild animals. We do not wish to domesticate them," DuBray said. The cooperative has "been trying to work with the Forest Service for years [to restore bison on grasslands], but the existing situation is that cattlemen have the [grazing] leases and they think they own it," he said.[14]

There may be one opportunity for a model compromise to bring three parties together—cattlemen, Forest Service, and the Standing Rock Sioux tribe—on the issue of the Cedar River NG in North Dakota. That small grassland is severely fragmented, with a limited wildlife management plan; scattered units are isolated in private and tribal land. The Forest Service should consider returning the land, acquired during the New Deal land purchases, to the tribe, but only after consulting permitees about land exchanges and future grazing leases with the tribe. Mike Claymore, acting tribal chief of the Standing Rock Sioux, said they would work with current grassland producers if the tribe had actual jurisdiction over the land. "We are not against the procedures there and we would agree to manage it the same as the Forest Service. They have a management scheme that works," he said. The tribe, according to Claymore, is more concerned that their reservation land was taken illegally, supposedly because it was submarginal, and they want it back.[15] The secretary of agriculture may be able to make the necessary changes administratively. A national grasslands trust fund could provide money to cover the costs of implementing a compromise, one that would go far toward suggesting solutions to other problems among competing parties elsewhere.

For many years, the highest purpose of the grasslands was to demonstrate range rehabilitation and good conservation practices. Thomas C. Nelson, deputy chief in charge of grasslands, reaffirmed this at a national grasslands workshop in 1979 when he deplored efforts to consolidate or "block-up" grasslands. He exclaimed, "I want this to stop! Our role is to encourage the integration of federally-owned lands into logical management units with the associated private lands. We can then use these units to favorably influence development of sound conservation practices in the whole area."[16]

Today Thomas Nelson is wrong. There are changes in management goals of the national grasslands, and that must now be recognized. There has already been some seventy years of demonstrating good conservation to neighboring ranchers and they have generally gotten the message by now. That "highest purpose" is now badly outmoded and the multiple purposes of national grasslands need to be recognized as the highest goals by top officials in Washington, as they often are down in the field at the district ranger level.

These changes will not come easily or quickly. They may take decades. If the policy changed overnight from grazing cattle to grazing bison on national grasslands, there would scarcely be enough bison in all of North America to make the switch. However, there are excellent opportunities to make a start:

Bison grazing should be allowed on the Little Missouri NG where it adjoins the Theodore Roosevelt National Park. Sometimes the

Park's bison stray onto the Grassland; they should not be shot for doing so, as is the occasional practice now.

Bison herds and prairie dog towns are growing on private, public, and reservation lands in the tri-corner area of South Dakota, Nebraska, and Wyoming. That can be expanded, with consolidation of diverse wildlife refuges there.

The small herd of three hundred to six hundred cattle on the Butte Valley NG can be eliminated, to allow full exploration of the immense wildlife possibilities there.

The only major tallgrass grassland reserve, on the Sheyenne River NG, cannot be effectively managed for multiple-use purposes with ten thousand head of cattle in numerous fenced allotments.

Many other opportunities abound. District rangers have shown great leadership in charting new concepts, as well as some frustration with the old rules that favor private cattle grazing. They should be encouraged to expand multiple-use management and gradually replace cattle with bison and other keystone species.

Today bison regularly stroll along highways in Custer State Park, South Dakota, and wander across them, while traffic stops and cameras click. That same lifetime experience can come, in time, to highways crossing the national grasslands.

27. Grasslands National Park in Saskatchewan, Canada, offers an environment of unobstructed views approaching how it used to be before human encroachment.

28. Prairie dogs on burrow, Grasslands National Park of Canada

Afterword

For many years, there has been a continuing argument between ranchers and conservationists—with the Forest Service in the middle—about black-tailed prairie dogs on the national grasslands. Ranchers don't want them because they eat too much grass and, especially in drought years, cause erosion and spread weeds. Conservationists see prairie dogs as a keystone species in the Great Plains, a vital link in the food chain for black-footed ferrets, raptors, swift fox, and other predators as well as providing essential support to bison, burrowing owls, and other species using their colonies.

That argument heated up in 2005, especially in the Conata Basin of the Buffalo Gap National Grassland and surrounding private lands. A long-term drought caused extensive expansion of prairie dog colonies, moving outside the grassland boundaries onto private land. Ranchers leasing grass-land acres complained about competition for scarce forage and ranches bordering the grassland became dotted with new prairie dog colonies.

South Dakota state legislators passed a state management plan to keep enough prairie dogs to prevent them from being listed as an endangered species, while providing funds to keep the animals off private lands where they are not wanted, through poisoning and other incentives.

The Forest Service developed its own management plan through an internal environmental impact statement (EIS) that provided for a half-mile buffer zone on both sides of the Buffalo Gap NG boundary, with tools including poisons, shooting, barrier fences, and grazing management to enforce the buffer. That EIS was approved and signed, but appeals were filed both by ranchers and conservationists. Those appeals were disallowed in November 2005 and a one-time program to eliminate prairie dogs within the buffer zone was to be completed by January 31, 2006.

The continuing controversy illustrates basic differences over how the grasslands should be used. Conservationists say that multiple use dictates a healthy and growing prairie dog population because so many other wildlife species depend upon them and their colonies. It also makes good economic sense, as wildlife viewing by the public becomes more and more popular. Prairie dog towns are well-established, permanent sites where people can see the wildlife every day, all day. In addition, both bison and cattle prefer to graze at those sites because there is new, tastier grass—there may be less biomass, but the quality is much better. In later years, prairie dog towns see more forbs emerge that attract other types of wildlife such as pronghorns.

Ranchers note that, especially with drought, the prairie dog towns have expanded much faster, as the animals seek out new forage areas. Spring winds, dry conditions, and bare grasslands caused by the colonies all combine to create dust-bowl conditions similar to the 1930s. In addition, prairie dogs bring on sylvatic plague, a deadly disease spread by fleas that kills prairie dogs and the black-footed ferrets that eat them. The plague can be deadly to humans, as well. Infected prairie dogs were found in 2005 on the Pine Ridge Indian Reservation, close to the Buffalo Gap NG and the area was dusted with insecticide.

This controversy has not affected the highly successful program to reintroduce black-footed ferrets on the Buffalo Gap NG. That decade-long program has a life of its own, with the animals now regenerating themselves into a healthy population, without the need of new implants.

Long-term solutions for this conflict will depend upon what funds become available. Poisons and rifles are only temporary answers. Barrier fences can prevent prairie dog migrations but they are expensive. Conservation easements that pay ranchers not to graze prairie dog acres would depend upon both public and private funds. Some conservation groups are exploring the idea of buying nearby ranches and then trading land or grazing rights with those ranchers affected by the invading colonies.

All of these ideas, and more, will be needed if this conflict is to be resolved. Fair weather, wet springs, and abundant grass will ease the situation, but the problem will still remain until real compromises can be found.

Photographer's Notes

Now for some interesting facts about this fifteen-month chunk of my life. All told, I drove over thirty thousand miles across North America. I shot over fifteen thousand images using my Canon 10D digital camera and Fuji 617 Panoramic film cameras. They never let me down, even though I did let them down (hard!) occasionally. Thank goodness for high-impact camera bodies.

I made it a practice of keeping a journal during my time on the road, and I thought a couple sections of it would shed some light on the process I go though when practicing my craft. Even though many people think I have the best job in the world (I'm not disagreeing), it is generally not pretty and is a ton of effort, just like any job done well. Anyway, with warts and all, here are some of my typical photographic days.

June 3, 2003, Oglala National Grassland

The light is fair and I shoot some images of cattle on grassland pastures, general scenics, and photos of abandoned buildings that was an underlying reason these grasslands were created. I wait impatiently for a final peek of sunshine under the clouds that have moved in, but it never comes. Such is the way it goes sometimes.

June 5, 2003, Buffalo Gap National Grassland

Starting to drag a bit. Eighteen-plus-hour days will do that to you. I have been skipping breakfast most mornings, and try to catch something to eat mid-morning unless I get busy again. I know, I know . . . it's stupid of me, but that's just the way it has worked out.

Started the morning in Buffalo Gap's Conata Basin shooting sunrise and the "magic pond" area (it has a thin layer of water over a clay base—great for reflection images). Came down the spine of Badlands National Park back into town to get gas and coffee (must—have—coffee). The only gas station has a torn-apart engine hanging in the lone service bay (looks like it had been there awhile), and the slowest gas pumps on the planet. No lids for the coffee cups. Asked the eighteen-something dude at the counter for one but he looked quite confused by my simple request. The lady-in-charge gets me one, but it ends up being the world's first "dribble" hot coffee lid (two drinking holes one right under the other!).

Not to complain, but constant travel mostly is a real pain in the arse. Romantic? Nah. Adventurous? At times. Hard days and not enough sleep? YES! I love my job.

A side note . . . I have taken many panoramic film photographs in the past three days. I feel like I have been capturing some nice shots, but I need to pace myself so I don't run out of large format film. Hope I'm right about the images or massive depression is in my future.

Reviewing digital images each night is a godsend. And having the opportunity for instant feedback is awesome, the best part about using a digital camera. Ooh! a KILLER shot of two avocets taking flight on the magic pond . . . cool!

June 6, 2003, South Dakota

Doubts . . . I have many doubts as to how I will ever be able to capture enough quality images for this project. I know getting shots that show how the areas look is doable, but I want to capture images that make you go "Wow." Most nights after reviewing shots on the laptop, I am gripped with the feeling that my efforts are not good enough, that I missed or blew golden photographic opportunities. These are the same feelings I get whenever I am working. My first impression of my images is always that they should have been better. I think this is because I want every image to be one I would be proud to hang in my gallery. I know this is unrealistic, but that is my nature. And looking at my efforts realistically, I have some really good images so far . . . but I want more, more, more!

It's now 10:30 p.m. Spent the entire day shooting at Grand River. What a nice place. Well marked, consolidated into sections, beautiful prairies. Arrived here about 11 a.m. and took images until the light was way past gone at 10 p.m. The campground where I am staying is hopping this Friday night. Don't know where all these people came from, but looks like they are here for the duration and they are enjoying themselves. There are golden oldies with all the toys, middle-agers with the kids AND the toys, the minimalists with just a car and tent, and a group of Metallica-playing, whoop it up high-schoolers congregated in the far corner of the campground . . . right where I am. Wonderful.

June 7, 2003

The high school crowd a few slots down from my campsite were going until I got up. Wish I had that much energy. Any-who, the noise of their festivities caused me a restless night. I was unable to roust myself at the appointed time of 4:30 a.m. as my eyes where glued shut. So I slept in until 4:45 a.m.

After much internal debate, finally decided to head over to the Sheyenne Grassland in eastern North Dakota, which is certainly different

from any of the other grasslands I have visited. Low sand hills, higher
foliage, many trees, ample water . . . and a bumper crop of mosquitoes.
This area seems to be hiding its secret places. My impression is that
one must really explore its many sections to fully comprehend what
is there. Things seem to be hiding just over that hill . . . or that one.
Unlike the other grasslands where you usually can get a high vantage
point coupled with low grass, this is just the opposite.

Better late than never, I finally get around to a meal (it's 10:45 p.m.).
I concoct an interesting mixture of Ro-tel, yellow peppers, pre-cooked
bacon, and snap peas. Not bad, not bad at all. Dang, I'm tired. Starting to make stupid mistakes. Ended up shooting for two hours with
the exposure compensation erroneously set to plus-one stop. I hate doing things like that. I have reached that point where I can't remember
clearly where I was or what I was doing earlier in my trip.

June 10, 2003, Little Missouri National Grassland

Reviewed the shots taken today. I am a dope, and my camera gear
should be taken away from me for everyone's protection. Sheesh.

It's 11 p.m., and the end of the day's work. I feel like I am treading
water, not accomplishing much of anything worthwhile. I usually feel
better in the morning and these thoughts go away. Usually.

After reading these journal thoughts, you may wonder why I do this. But
the funny thing is, I truly enjoy my profession. The rigors of the road are
more than offset by the experiences I have had as I travel around this great
world of ours. The sublime beauty of the coming morning, the incredible
sunrises and sunsets I have witnessed, and the feeling of being one with nature. It makes it all worthwhile. I truly appreciate the opportunity to practice my craft on a daily basis.

I hope that after viewing the images in this book, you will feel some of the
joy I felt when I originally took the photograph. If so, then I have achieved
what I set out to do.

Notes

1. *"No Darker Chapter nor Greater Tragedy"*

1. John C. Hudson, *Making the Corn Belt: A Geographical History of Middle-Western Agriculture* (Bloomington: Indiana University Press, 1994), 1.

2. John C. Hoyt, *Droughts of 1930–34* (Washington DC: U.S. Government Printing Office, 1936), 2.

3. R. G. Barry, "Climatic Environment of the Great Plains, Past and Present," in *Man and the Changing Environments in the Great Plains*, ed. Warren W. Caldwell, C. Bertrand Schultz, and T. Myland Stout, 45 (Lincoln: Transactions of the Nebraska Academy of Sciences, 1983).

4. Harry E. Weakly, "History of Drought in Nebraska," *Journal of Soil and Water Conservation* 17 (November–December 1962): 272.

5. Barry, "Climatic Environment," 49.

6. H. C. Fritts, "Tree-ring Dating and Reconstructed Variations in Central Plains Climate," in *Man and the Changing Environments in the Great Plains*, ed. Warren Caldwell, C. Bertrand Schultz, and T. Myland Stout, 39 (Lincoln: Transactions of the Nebraska Academy of Sciences, 1983).

7. J. E. Weaver and F. W. Albertson, *Grasslands of the Great Plains* (Lincoln: Johnsen Publishing, 1956), 75.

8. Weaver and Albertson, *Grasslands*, 76.

9. Weaver and Albertson, *Grasslands*, 76.

10. Donald Worster, *Dust Bowl: The Southern Plains in the 1930s* (New York: Oxford University Press, 1979), 13.

11. Worster, *Dust Bowl*, 13.

12. Henry A. Wallace, *The Western Range: Letter from the Secretary of Agriculture Transmitting in Response to Senate Resolution No. 289 a Report on the Western Range—A Great but Neglected Natural Resource* (Washington DC: U.S. Government Printing Office, 1936), 3.

13. Henry A. Wallace, *Western Range*, 8.

14. Henry C. Wallace, *Secretary of Agriculture Annual Report 1923* (Washington DC: U.S. Government Printing Office, 1923), 72–77.

15. Paul W. Gates, *History of Public Land Law Development* (Washington DC: U.S. Government Printing Office, U.S. Public Land Law Review Commission, 1968), 522.

16. Gates, *Public Land Law Development*, 524.

17. Arthur Hyde, *Proceedings of the National Conference on Land Utilization, Chicago IL, November 19–21, 1931* (Washington DC: U.S. Government Printing Office, 1932), 2.

18. Hyde, *Conference on Land Utilization*, 3–6.

19. Hyde, *Conference on Land Utilization*, 17–23.

20. Hyde, *Conference on Land Utilization*, 26.

21. Albert Z. Guttenburg, "The Land Utilization Movement of the 1920s," *Agricultural History* 3 (July 1976): 481.

22. Hyde, *Conference on Land Utilization*, 242–45.

2. *Land, the First Essential*

1. Addison E. Sheldon, *Land Systems and Land Policies in Nebraska* (Lincoln: Nebraska State Historical Society, 1936), 1.

2. L. C. Gray, quoted in Henry C. Wallace, *Agriculture Annual Report 1923*, 415.

3. John Wesley Powell, *Report on the Lands of the Arid Region of the United States* (Washington DC: U.S. Government Printing Office, 1879), 20–22.

4. Guttenburg, "Land Utilization Movement," 477.

5. Guttenberg, "Land Utilization Movement," 477.

6. Guttenberg, "Land Utilization Movement," 480.

7. Guttenberg, "Land Utilization Movement," 481.

8. Paul Bonnifield, *The Dust Bowl: Men, Dirt, and Depression* (Albuquerque: University of New Mexico Press, 1979), 111.

9. Guttenburg, "Land Utilization Movement," 480.

10. Bonnifield, *Men, Dirt, and Depression*, 70.

11. Paul K. Conkin, *Tomorrow a New World: The New Deal Community Program* (Ithaca NY: Cornell University

Press, 1957), 76–77.

12. Conkin, *Tomorrow a New World*, 77.

13. Conkin, *Tomorrow a New World*, 77.

14. Frederick W. Obermiller, "The Evolution of Regulated Livestock Grazing Systems on the National Grasslands" (paper presented at the Great Plains Grasslands Eighteenth Annual Interdisciplinary Symposium, University of Nebraska–Lincoln, April 8, 1994, 3).

15. Conkin, *Tomorrow a New World*, 34.

16. Bernard Sternsher, *Rexford Tugwell and the New Deal* (New Brunswick NJ: Rutgers University Press, 1964), 267.

17. Conkin, *Tomorrow a New World*, 83.

3. *A Strange and Dramatic Moment*

1. R. G. Tugwell, *The Brains Trust* (New York: Viking Press, 1968), 183.

2. Richard S. Kirkendall, *Social Scientists and Farm Politics in the Age of Roosevelt* (Columbia: University of Missouri Press, 1966), 54.

3. Gladys Baker et al., *Century of Service: The First 100 Years of the United States Department of Agriculture* (Washington DC: Government Printing Office, 1963), 247.

4. Kirkendall, *Social Scientists and Farm Politics*, 42

5. Conkin, *Tomorrow a New World*, 149.

6. Conkin, *Tomorrow a New World*, 149.

7. Conkin, *Tomorrow a New World*, 152.

8. H. H. Wooten, *The Land Utilization Program, 1934 to 1964: Origin, Development, and Present Status* (Washington DC: U.S. Department of Agriculture, Economic Research Service, 1965), 5.

9. Kirkendall, *Social Scientists and Farm Politics*, 56–7.

10. Wooten, *Land Utilization Program*, 5.

11. Wooten, *Land Utilization Program*, 5.

12. Wooten, *Land Utilization Program*, 5–6.

13. Wooten, *Land Utilization Program*, 6.

14. Wooten, *Land Utilization Program*, 6–7.

15. Wooten, *Land Utilization Program*, 8.

16. Wooten, *Land Utilization Program*, 8–10.

17. Conkin, *Tomorrow a New World*, 88.

18. Conkin, *Tomorrow a New World*, 89.

19. Conkin, *Tomorrow a New World*, 98.

20. Conkin, *Tomorrow a New World*, 109.

21. Conkin, *Tomorrow a New World*, 114–15.

22. Sternsher, *Rexford Tugwell*, 264.

23. Gates, *Public Land Law Development*, 611.

24. Gates, *Public Land Law Development*, 618.

25. Sternsher, *Rexford Tugwell*, 265.

26. Sternsher, *Rexford Tugwell*, 268.

27. Sternsher, *Rexford Tugwell*, 268.

28. Sternsher, *Rexford Tugwell*, 269.

29. Sternsher, *Rexford Tugwell*, 271–72.

30. Sternsher, *Rexford Tugwell*, 273.

31. Wooten, *Land Utilization Program*, 10.

32. Wooten, *Land Utilization Program*, 11.

33. Sternsher, *Rexford Tugwell*, 273.

34. Sternsher, *Rexford Tugwell*, 273.

35. Wooten, *Land Utilization Program*, 10.

36. Wooten, *Land Utilization Program*, 10.

37. Sternsher, *Rexford Tugwell*, 274–76.

38. Sternsher, *Rexford Tugwell*, 277–78.

39. Sternsher, *Rexford Tugwell*, 279.

40. Sternsher, *Rexford Tugwell*, 281.

41. Sternsher, *Rexford Tugwell*, 282.

42. Conkin, *Tomorrow a New World*, 178–79.

43. Sternsher, *Rexford Tugwell*, 296.

44. Tyler Sutton, "Laying the Groundwork for a Great Grassland Preserve: Some Preliminary Considerations" (unpublished paper, Conservational Alliance of the Great Plains, January 1, 2002, 8). Paper on file with author.

45. R. Douglas Hurt, "The National Grasslands: Origin and Development in the Dust Bowl," in *The History of Soil and Water Conservation*, ed. Douglas Helms and Susan L. Flader, 147 (Washington DC: Agricultural History Society, 1985).

46. Hurt, "National Grasslands," 156–57.

47. Wooten, *Land Utilization Program*, 17–18.

4. Broken-up Badlands, Thin Threads of Trees

1. James C. Olson, *History of Nebraska* (Lincoln: University of Nebraska Press, 1965), 286–90.

2. *Harrison (NE) Sun*, October 24, 1935.

3. *Harrison Sun*, November 14, 1935.

4. *Harrison Sun*, October 31, 1935.

5. *Harrison Sun*, December 23, 1937.

6. E. P. Wilson, "Brief History of Dawes County," in *Pioneer Tales of the North Platte Valley and Nebraska Panhandle*, ed. Asa Butler Wood, 204 (Gering NE: Courier Press, 1938).

7. *Harrison Sun*, September 29, 1938.

8. All quotations and information concerning Oglala National Grassland purchases come from U.S. Forest Service, *Land Purchases of the Oglala National Grassland*, microfiche files, Chadron NE, 1936–41.

9. Albert Meng, retired rancher, personal interview, Crawford NE, March 22, 1994.

10. Carroll Schnurr, letter to Francis Moul, February 25, 1994.

11. Obermiller, "Evolution of Regulated Livestock Grazing Systems," 11.

12. *Harrison Sun*, April 27, 1939.

13. *Harrison Sun*, December 5, 1940.

14. U.S. Forest Service, *Grazing Association Plan: Sugarloaf Grazing Association and Oglala National Grassland* (Chadron NE: U.S. Forest Service, 1987), 1–5.

15. Butch Ellis, U.S. Forest Service manager, personal interview, Chadron NE, March 21, 1994.

16. Wes Pettipiece, rancher, personal interview, rural Harrison NE, March 22, 1994.

5. Highest Purpose of the Grasslands

1. O. J. Reichman, *Konza Prairie: A Tallgrass Natural History* (Lawrence: University Press of Kansas, 1987), 20.

2. Reichman, *Konza Prairie*, 21.

3. Douglas B. Bamforth, *Ecology and Human Organization on the Great Plains* (Lincoln: University of Nebraska Press, 1988), 58.

4. Ronald C. Tobey, *Saving the Prairies: The Life Cycle of the Founding School of American Plant Ecology, 1895–1955* (Berkeley: University of California Press, 1981), 192–4; italics added.

5. Tobey, *Saving the Prairies*, 196–8.

6. Obermiller, "Evolution of Regulated Livestock Grazing Systems," 16.

7. Wooten, *Land Utilization Program*, 31.

8. Hurt, "National Grasslands," 151–52.

9. William D. Rowley, *U.S. Forest Service Grazing and Rangelands: A History* (College Station: Texas A&M University Press, 1985), 169.

10. James Stubbendieck, professor of Range Ecology and Agronomy, University of Nebraska–Lincoln, phone interview, May 19, 2004.

11. Rowley, *Grazing and Rangelands*, 166–67.

12. Rowley, *Grazing and Rangelands*, 178.

13. Rowley, *Grazing and Rangelands*, 184.

14. Rowley, *Grazing and Rangelands*, 205–06.

15. Rowley, *Grazing and Rangelands*, 206–07.

16. Rowley, *Grazing and Rangelands*, 226.

17. Rowley, *Grazing and Rangelands*, 231.

18. Rowley, *Grazing and Rangelands*, 233.

19. Rowley, *Grazing and Rangelands*, 237–38.

20. Rowley, *Grazing and Rangelands*, 238–39.

21. Leslie Aileen Duram, "The National Grasslands: Past, Present, and Future Land Management Issues," *Rangelands* 17 (April 1995): 41.

22. All quotes are from Terry West, "USDA Forest Service Management of the National Grasslands" (unpaginated paper prepared for the Symposium on the United States Department of Agriculture in Historical Perspective, Iowa State University (Ames), June 15–18, 1989).

23. Pete Read, "Stewardship of the Crooked River National Grassland," *National Grasslands Forum Proceedings* (Billings MT: Custer National Forest, 1989), 35–36.

Part II. A Guide to the National Grasslands

1. *Introduction to the Crooked River National Grassland* (unpaginated, undated brochure).

2. Kristin M. Bail, district ranger, phone interview, Madras OR, June 4, 2004.

3. Kristin Bail, *Crooked River National Grassland Vegetation Management-Grazing Environmental Impact Statement* (Crooked River National Grassland, Jefferson County OR, April 5, 2004), 1.

4. Coleen H. Swetten Jr., *Curlew National Grassland* (unpublished paper, 1980), 6.

5. "Development Story, Curlew National Grassland, Malad Ranger District" (unpublished report, no date), 2.

6. Rick VanBebben, rangeland manager, personal interview, Malad ID, May 23, 1996.

7. Ken Timothy, wildlife biologist, phone interview, Malad ID, June 9, 2004.

8. "Development Story, Curlew National Grassland," 4–5.

9. Rick VanBebben, interagency noxious weed coordinator, phone interview, Malad ID, June 14, 2004.

10. Twyla Browning, range ecologist, personal interview, Macdoel CA, May 20, 1996.

11. Jim Stout, resource officer, phone interview, Macdoel CA, June 15, 2004.

12. Jay Carlisle, "Butte Valley National Grassland Bird Report 1995–1996" (unpublished report, Butte Valley National Grassland, Macdoel CA, 1996).

13. Gary Foli, wildlife biologist, phone interview, Watford City ND, June 16, 2004.

14. Curt Hansen, range conservationist, personal interview, Lisbon ND, May 31, 1996.

15. *Sheyenne National Grassland* (brochure, Lisbon ND, no date), 1.

16. *Western Prairie Fringed Orchid* (brochure, Minnesota Natural Heritage Program Section of Wildlife, Minnesota Department of Natural Resources, 1991), 1–6.

17. Bryan Stotts, district ranger, phone interview, Lisbon ND, June 17, 2004.

18. Bob Anderson, range technician, phone interview, Lemmon SD, June 18, 2004.

19. Dan Svingen, wildlife biologist, phone interview, Lemmon SD, June 18, 2004.

20. Forest Morin, range manager, personal interview, Lemmon SD, May 30, 1996.

21. Tom Domek, *The National Grasslands Story: From Dust Bowl to Public Prairies* (no publisher, no date), 20.

22. Svingen, interview, June 18, 2004.

23. *The Lemmon Aide* (Lemmon SD: Print Shop, 1994), 8–18.

24. Doug Stewart, "Caught in a Dog Fight," *National Wildlife* 37 (June/July 1999): 36–9.

25. Glenn Moravek, wildlife biologist, phone interview, Pierre SD, June 26, 2004.

26. Tonya Weisbeck, range conservation specialist, phone interview, Pierre SD, June 22, 2004.

27. Bill Perry, district ranger, personal interview, Wall SD, April 13, 2004.

28. *Nebraska's Threatened and Endangered Species, Black-Footed Ferret* (brochure, Nebraska Game and Park Commission, no date), 1–3.

29. Bob Hodorff, wildlife biologist, phone interview, Hot Springs SD, June 24, 2004.

30. Mike Erk, range conservation specialist, phone interview, Hot Springs SD, June 24, 2004.

31. Bill Perry, district ranger, phone interview, Wall SD, June 25, 2004.

32. Gary Besco, "Hot Springs District of the Buffalo Gap National Grasslands" (master's thesis, University of South Dakota, 1995).

33. Dan O'Brien, rancher and author, personal interview, rural Hermosa SD, April 12, 2004.

34. Charlie Marsh, district ranger, phone interview, Chadron NE, June 25, 2004.

35. Jeff Abegglen, wildlife biologist, phone interview, Chadron NE, June 25, 2004.

36. Bruce Sprentall, district ranger, phone interview, Douglas WY, June 30, 2004.

37. Bruce Ramsey, assistant director of minerals and geology, U.S. Forest Service, phone interview, Washington DC, May 13, 2004.

38. Cecile Gray, administration project leader, forest management and rangeland management, U.S. Forest Service, phone interview, Washington DC, May 13, 2004.

39. Mary Peterson, forest supervisor, phone interview, Laramie WY, March 16, 2004.

40. *Visitor Guide, Medicine Bow–Routt National Forests, Thunder Basin National Grassland* (brochure, U.S. Forest Service, no date), 2. See also, *Thunder Basin National Grassland Map* (U.S. Forest Service, 2003).

41. Beth Humphrey, wildlife biologist, phone interview, Greeley CO, July 9, 2004.

42. Randy Reichert, range conservation specialist, phone interview, Greeley CO, July 9, 2004.

43. *Mammals, Flora, and Fauna of the Pawnee National Grassland* (brochure, U.S. Forest Service, Greeley CO, August 2002).

44. Tom Peters, district ranger, phone interview, Springfield CO, June 30, 2004.

45. Dave Augustine, wildlife biologist, phone interview, Springfield CO, June 30, 2004.

46. Andy Chappell, wildlife biologist, phone interview, Elkhart KS, July 7, 2004.

47. Nancy Brewer, rangeland management specialist, phone interview, Elkhart KS, July 7, 2004.

48. Nancy Walls, district manager, phone interview, Clayton NM, July 13, 2004.

49. Darrell Musick, range conservationist, personal interview, Clayton NM, March 14, 1997.

50. Tom Smeltzer, natural resources specialist, phone interview, Cheyenne OK, July 16, 2004.

51. Chuck Milner, range management specialist, phone interview, Cheyenne OK, July 14, 2004.

52. Jim Crooks, district ranger, phone interview, Decatur TX, July 16, 2004.

53. Claire Curry, *Butterfly Checklist, Wise County, Texas* (pamphlet, no publisher, July 13, 2003).

54. Claire Curry, *Bird Checklist, Wise County, Texas* (pamphlet, Tallgrass Prairie Audubon Society, Decatur TX, June 2003).

55. Pat Fargey, wildlife biologist, phone interview, Val Marie, Saskatchewan, Canada, July 22, 2004.

56. Rick Caples, acting deputy chief, National Grasslands, U.S. Forest Service, phone interview, Washington DC, July 7, 2004.

Part III. Bison Instead of Cattle?

1. Dan O'Brien, *Buffalo for the Broken Heart: Restoring Life to a Black Hills Ranch* (New York: Random House, 2001), 217–18.

2. Rick Caples, phone interview, July 7, 2004.

3. Bill Perry, district ranger, phone interview, Wall SD, August 9, 2004.

4. Nate Skjoldal, president, Association of National Grasslands, phone interview, Lemmon SD, July 27, 2004.

5. *Bankhead-Jones Farm Tenant Act*, Seventy-fifth Congress, 1st Session, CHS.517, July 22, 1937.

6. Morris Hankins, attorney in charge, Office of General Counsel, U.S. Department of Agriculture, letter to Regional Forester, October 25, 1978, from *National Grasslands 1981 Information Handbook, Custer National Forest*.

7. True D. Morse, acting secretary of agriculture, *Secretary's Administrative Order of June 23, 1960, Title 36, Parks, Forests, and Memorials*, U.S. Department of Agriculture, Washington DC, from *National Grasslands 1981 Information Handbook, Custer National Forest*.

8. Sutton, "Laying the Groundwork for a Great Grassland Preserve," 27–8.

9. Daniel Licht, *Ecology and Economics of the Great Plains* (Lincoln: University of Nebraska Press, 1997), 90–91.

10. S. C. Forrest et al., *Ocean of Grass: A Conservation Assessment for the Northern Great Plains* (Bozeman MT: Northern Plains Conservation Network, 2004), 103–4.

11. Forrest et al., *Ocean of Grass*, 4.

12. Tyler Sutton, president, Great Plains Conservation Alliance, personal interview, Lincoln NE, June 25, 2004.

13. Butch Ellis, field director, The Nature Conservancy, personal interview, Chadron NE, June 28, 2004

14. Fred DuBray, president, Intertribal Bison Cooperative, phone interview, Rapid City SD, July 27, 2004.

15. Mike Claymore, acting tribal chief, Standing Rock Sioux, phone interview, Fort Yates ND, July 30, 2004.

16. Thomas C. Nelson, deputy chief, U.S. Forest Service, address to National Grasslands Workshop, no place, December 1979, from *National Grasslands 1981 Information Handbook, Custer National Forest*.

Index

Abegglen, Jeff, 86
agrarian fundamentalism, 25
Agricultural Adjustment Act of 1933,
   26–28
agriculture: Conservation Reserve
   Program (CRP), 124; drought
   and introduction of, 12; farm
   commodity prices and, 37–38;
   Great Depression and, 13–16, 23;
   homestead vs. ranching struggle,
   13; land repurchase programs in,
   26–30; land use policy and, 19–20,
   124; New Deal relief programs, 21;
   parity pricing in, 15, 26; Resettlement Administration and, 32–35;
   subsidies and transfer payments,
   20, 119–20
Alexander, Will W., 31

Altithermal. *See* drought
Anderson, Bob, 73
Angastura Reservoir (South Dakota),
   80
animals: grasslands introduction of,
   2–3; grasslands reintroduction of,
   57, 60, 62, 67, 79–80, 112; Ice Age
   migrations of, 3–4. *See also* bison;
   black-footed ferret; endangered
   species; livestock industry; prairie
   dogs; wildlife preservation
animal units per month (AUM), 43–44,
   120–21. *See also* grazing permits
archaeological sites. *See* Comanche
   National Grassland; Grand River
   National Grassland; Little Missouri National Grassland; Oglala
   National Grassland

Association of National Grassland Associations, 84

Association of National Grasslands (ANG), 84, 122

Augustine, Dave, 97

back-to-the-land movements, 20–22, 25

Badlands National Park, 21, 80, 127, 136

Bail, Kristin M., 60

Bamforth, Douglas, 46

Bankhead-Jones Farm Tenant Act of 1937, 35, 47, 52, 123–24

Barbour, W. Warren, 34

Barr, Claude, 82

Barrett, Frank A., 49

Beam, Arlen, 120–21

biodiversity, 123–30

bison: Buffalo Commons concept and, 119; at Buffalo Gap NG, 84; drought cycles and, 12; at Fort Pierre NG, 79–80; at Grasslands National Park of Canada, 111; grasslands origins and, 4; herd psyche of, 117–18; Intertribal Bison Cooperative and, 128; at Little Missouri NG, 69; multiple use programs and, 124–30

black-footed ferret, 80–82, 120, 122, 127, 131–33

Black Hills National Forest, 80–81, 127

Black Kettle National Grassland (Oklahoma, Texas), 103–5; controlled burns in, 104; ecosystem of, 105; grazing allotments in, 104; map of, 105; natural resources in, 104; origin of name, 105; recreational uses in, 104; wildlife habitat of, 103

blocking up, 80–81. *See also* consolidation

Boe, Deen, 52

boreal forests, 45–46

Browning, Twyla, 65

buffalo. *See* bison

Buffalo Commons concept, 119

Buffalo Gap National Grassland (South Dakota), 80–84, 136; agricultural relief programs and, 21; biodiversity restoration in, 127; bison grazing permits in, 118; black-footed ferret reintroduction in, 120; map of, 81; National Grasslands Visitor Center at, 58; Oglala NG and, 37; prairie dogs in, 131–33; tourism in, 80

burns, controlled, 53, 60, 62, 69, 72, 77, 104

Butte Valley National Grassland (California), 63–65; dedication of, 36; map of, 64,; grazing allotments in, 65; as L-U project, 47, 63; management alternatives in, 130

Butte Valley Wildlife Area, 64

Caddo National Grassland (Texas), 107–9; ecosystem of, 109; historic restoration in, 107; map of, 108; recreational uses in, 107; tourism in, 107

California. *See* Butte Valley National Grassland

Canada: Grasslands National Park, 111–14; Ocean of Grass conservation assessment, 127; Protected Heritage System, 111

Caples, Rick, 113, 120

Carlisle, Jay, 65

Cascade Mountains, 58, 65

cattle. *See* livestock industry

Cedar River National Grassland (North Dakota), 73–74; ecosystem of, 73; future alternatives for, 128–29; grazing allotments in, 74; map of, 73; reseeding management in, 73–74; Standing Rock Reservation and, 74; wildlife habitat in, 74

Central South Dakota Grazing District v. U.S. Forest Service, 120–21

Chadron NE, 43, 82, 128

Chadron State College (Nebraska), 82

Cimarron National Grassland (Kansas), 97–99; consolidation of, 91, 98; grazing allotments in, 99; map of, 98; recreational uses in, 99; reseeding management in, 99; Santa Fe Trail and, 91, 97

Civilian Conservation Corps, 86, 107

Claymore, Mike, 128–29

climate: Cascade Mountains impact on, 58; climax species and, 46–47; Rocky Mountains impact on, 1–4, 11–12, 45

climax theory, 46–47

coal mining, 87. *See also* natural resources

Colorado. *See* Comanche National Grassland; Pawnee National Grassland

Comanche National Grassland (Colorado), 92, 94–97; archaeological sites in, 94–97; grazing allotments in, 97; map of, 95; natural resources in, 97

conservation: human intervention in, 47; L-U project "land grab" and, 49–50. *See also* Bankhead-Jones Farm Tenant Act of 1937; Multiple Use-Sustained Yield Act of 1960

Conservation Reserve Program (CRP), 124

consolidation, 91, 123–30. *See also* blocking up

"cool burns." *See* burns, controlled

cover crops, 48

Crooked River National Grassland (Oregon), 58–60; controlled burns in, 53, 60; map of, 59; grazing allotments in, 52–54; tourism in, 60

Crooks, Jim, 109

Cross Timbers National Grassland. *See* Lyndon B. Johnson National Grassland

Curlew National Grassland (Idaho), 60–63; controlled burns in, 62; map of, 61; native bird habitat in, 57, 62–63; recreational uses in, 63; reseeding management in, 62; tourism in, 60, 62–63

Custer, George, 70, 76, 105, 113

Custer State Park (South Dakota), 21, 80–81, 127, 130

DeVoto, Bernard, 49

Dirty Thirties, 5–6, 12

Drifter Cookshack, 86

drought: Altithermal, 4, 12; Dirty Thirties and, 5–6; farm commodity prices and, 37–38; and fire precautions, 86–87; grasses as climax species in, 46–47; grasslands origins from, 4; and grazing restrictions, 120–21; causes of, 11–12; tree-ring studies of, 12

DuBray, Fred, 128

Duram, Leslie Aileen, 51

dust storms, 13–14

ecosystem management, 120–30

Ellis, Butch, 43, 128

Emergency Relief Act of 1935, 34

Emergency Relief Administration, 21–22

endangered species: black-footed ferret, 80–82, 120, 122, 127, 131; butterflies, 72, 82; of Canada, 112; mountain plovers, 92; of Oglala NG, 86; prairie dogs as, 131–32; reintroduction of, 57; swift fox, 79, 82, 94, 100; western prairie white-fringed orchid, 72; whooping cranes and bald eagles, 77. *See also* Turner Endangered Species Fund; wildlife preservation

Endangered Species Act of 1973, 51

energy resources. *See* grasslands management; natural resources

environment: grasslands management and, 5–7; grasslands origins and, 1–4; impact of drought on, 11–12; National Environmental Protection Act of 1969, 50

environmental impact statements (EIS): for mining and drilling, 91, 50–51; for prairie dog, 132. *See also* National Environmental Protection Act of 1969

environmental studies, 18–20

Erk, Mike, 83

erosion: drought and, 13–14; grasslands origins from, 1–3; land repurchase and, 26–30, 38–39; reseeding for, 62; soil rehabilitation from, 48. *See also* soil conservation

family farms, 15–16, 20–21, 32–35, 119–20

Fargey, Pat, 111

Farm Credit Administration, 37–38

Farm Home Administration, 64

farming. *See* agriculture

Farm Security Administration, 35, 39

Federal Emergency Relief Administration (FERA), 26, 28

Federal Farm Board, 16

federal government. *See* U.S. Government

Federal Land Policy and Management Act of 1976, 51

fire. *See* burns, controlled; wild fires

Foli, Gary, 69–70

Forbes, William M., 40

forest to grassland transition, 2, 45–46

Fort Pierre National Grassland (South Dakota), 77–80; controlled burns in, 77; endangered species of, 77–79; grazing allotments in, 79–80; grazing permits in, 120–21; map of, 78

Fort Robinson State Park (Nebraska), 85–86

fossils and historical sites. *See* archaeological sites; history, grasslands

glaciation, 1–4, 45, 72. *See also* Ice Age

Glass, Hugh, 76–77

Grand River National Grassland (South Dakota), 75–77; archaeological sites in, 76–77; map of, 75; recreational uses in, 76; wildlife habitat in, 75–76. *See also* Cedar River National Grasslands

Grassland Foundation, 127

grasslands biome, 46

grasslands management: animal units per month (AUM), 43–44; controversy and debate in, 6–7, 131–33; and energy resources, 6–7; environmental impact statements of (EIS), 50–51; future alternatives for, 120–30; land ownership and, 15, 49–51; multiple use philosophy of,

48–49; New Deal transformation of, 5–6, 118–20; U.S. Forest Service and, 35–36; vegetational succession in, 45–47; water rights and, 18–19; wilderness areas and, 84. *See also* Bankhead-Jones Farm Tenant Act of 1937; burns, controlled; Endangered Species Act of 1973; Federal Land Policy and Management Act of 1976; Public Rangelands Improvement Act of 1978; reseeding management; Sugarloaf Soil Conservation District

Grasslands National Park of Canada, 111–14; and historic relevance, 113; recreational uses, 112; tourism in, 112–13

Grasslands Reserve Program, 124

grass species: blue bunch grass, 60; bluebunch wheatgrass, 52–53; blue grama grass, 48, 74, 77, 93, 104; bluegrass, 62, 65, 69, 72; bluestem, big and little, 48, 74, 77, 103–4, 109; brome grass, 72, 87; buffalo grass, 2–3, 48, 77, 93, 103; bunch grass, 60; cheatgrass, 65, 87; crested wheatgrass, 47–48, 60, 62, 65, 69, 74, 93; Idaho fescue, 60, 65; Indian grass, 104, 109; needle grasses, 65, 69, 74, 77, 87; sideoats grama, 48, 77, 103–4; Sudan grass, 48; switch grass, 104; western wheatgrass, 48, 69, 74, 77, 87, 93

Gray, Cecile, 88

Gray, Lewis C., 18–19, 27, 33

grazing allotments: burning to increase, 53–54; prairie adaptations to, 46–47; semi-arid mixed prairie, 46. *See also* Black Kettle NG; Buffalo Gap NG; Butte Valley NG; Cedar River NG; Cimarron NG; Comanche NG; Crooked River NG; Fort Pierre NG; Grasslands National Park of Canada; Kiowa NG; Little Missouri NG; Lyndon B. Johnson NG; Oglala NG; Pawnee NG; Rita Blanca NG; reseeding management; Sheyenne River NG; Thunder Basin NG

grazing associations: in Buffalo Gap NG, 83–84; grasslands management by, 47–48, 52, 121–23. *See also* Sugarloaf Grazing Association

grazing districts, 35–36, 42–43, 49–50

grazing permits: animal units and, 43–44; for bison, 80, 84, 118, 129–30; drought and, 120–21; grasslands management and, 6–7, 47–48; L-U project "land grab" and, 49; politics and, 123–30. *See also* livestock industry

Great Depression: agriculture and, 13–14, 23; drought cycles and, 12; economic causes of, 25; farm commodity prices in, 37–38; Great Plains transformation during, 5–6, 118–20

Great Plains: American history and, 17–18, 60; Buffalo Commons concept of, 118–20; drought and Dust Bowl era in, 11–16; forest to grassland transition in, 45; grass adaptations in, 46–47; grasslands origins of, 1–4; L-U projects in, 47–48; New Deal transformation of, 5–6. *See also* Northern Great Plains; Ocean of Grass conservation assessment; Ogallala Aquifer; Southern Great Plains

Guttenberg, Albert Z., 19

Hansen, Curt, 70

herbicides, 53, 87, 97, 104

high desert, 58

history, grasslands: settlement and land ownership in, 17–18

Hodorff, Bob, 82

Homestead Act, 22

homesteading: grasslands depletion and, 14–15; public lands conflict and, 13; Taylor Grazing Act of 1934 and, 16; water rights and, 19; withdrawal of lands from, 30

Hoover, Herbert, 15, 23

Hudson, John, 11

human habitation: drought impact on, 12; grassland role in, 3–4; impact on climax prairie, 46–47; impact on Great Plains environment, 13–16; increased grasslands use from, 60; land ownership and, 17

Humphrey, Beth, 92

hunting, 62–63

Ice Age, 1–4, 12, 45. *See also* glaciation

Ickes, Harold L., 29

Indian reservations: land use planning and, 128–29; New Deal L-U projects for, 26; Resettlement Administration and, 32–35. *See also* Lower Brule Indian Reservation; Pine Ridge Indian Reservation; Standing Rock Reservation; Warm Springs Reservation

Indian rock art, 95–96

Intertribal Bison Cooperative, 128

invasive plant species: broom snakeweed, 87; Canada thistle, 72, 77, 87, 93; dyer's woad, 63; herbicides and, 53, 87, 97, 104; Japanese brome, 87; juniper and sagebrush, 52–53;

Kentucky bluegrass, 69, 72; leafy spurge and knapweeds, 63, 69, 72, 93; salt cedar, 93, 97; Scotch thistle, 104; sickle weed, 77. *See also* weeds
irrigation, 15–16, 18–20

Jardine, W. M., 15
Jeffersonian agrarian philosophy, 25

Kansas. *See* Cimarron National Grassland
Kiowa National Grassland (New Mexico), 101–3; grazing allotments in, 103; map of, 102; Santa Fe Trail in, 103; wildlife habitat in, 101–2
Klamath National Forest (California), 36, 64

Land and Water Conservation Fund, 126
land classification, 19–20, 31, 48
land exchanges, 80–81, 91, 123–30
Land Policy Section (Agricultural Adjustment Administration), 27–28
land purchase programs: future alternatives for, 123–30; goal of federal, 38–41; government misrepresentation in, 42; tenant-rehabilitation and, 20–21. *See also* Farm Credit Administration; New Deal
land surveys, 21, 28
Land Systems and Land Policies in Nebraska (Sheldon), 17
land use: alternatives, 120–30; Bureau of Agricultural Economics and, 19–20; federal policy toward, 15–16; land ownership and, 17–18, 49–51, 128–30; New Deal reforms in, 25–30; Resettlement Administration and, 30–35; resettlement programs

in, 20–21; western settlement and, 18–19. *See also* L-U (land utilization) projects
Licht, Daniel, 125
Little Missouri National Grassland (North Dakota), 67–70; archaeological sites in, 70; bison grazing in, 69, 129–30; conservation assessment of, 127; and Lewis and Clark, 69–70; map of, 66, 68; natural resources of, 70; recreational uses in, 67, 69–70; tourism in, 70
livestock industry: Buffalo Commons concept and, 119; during drought and Dust Bowl era, 14–16, 41; grasslands future uses and, 120–30; homesteading and, 13; impact on weed control, 53; L-U project "land grab" and, 49–51; public lands and the, 12–13. *See also* animal units per month; Federal Land Policy and Management Act of 1976; Public Rangelands Improvement Act of 1978
Louisiana Purchase of 1803, 18
Lower Brule Indian Reservation, 77–78
L-U (land utilization) projects: and Agricultural Adjustment Administration, 26–30; Butte Valley NG as, 47, 63; federal control of, 35–36; Forest Service management of, 48–50; grasslands development and, 47–48; management of, 121; Nebraska land purchases, 37–44. *See also* land use
Lyndon B. Johnson National Grassland (Texas), 109–11; grazing allotments in, 111; map of, 100; natural resources of, 111; recreational uses in, 109–10; wildlife habitat in, 110–11

Marsh, Charlie, 85
McClellan Creek National Grassland (Texas), 92, 106–7; map of, 106; recreational uses at, 92, 106–7
Mead, Elwood, 15
Medicine Bow National Forest, 91
Meng, Albert, 41–43, 86
Meng, Helen, 41
Milner, Check, 104
mineral extraction. *See* natural resources
mineral rights. *See* natural resources
mining. *See* natural resources
Mississippi River, 2
Missouri River, 1–2, 77–80, 90
mixed-grass prairie, 45–47. *See also* grass species
Montana: land use experiments in, 20–21; livestock industry in, 13; L-U projects in, 35. *See also* Intertribal Bison Cooperative
Moravek, Glenn, 77
Mount Shasta CA, 65
Multiple Use–Sustained Yield Act of 1960, 50, 123
Musick, Darrell, 102

National Environmental Protection Act of 1969, 50
national forests: administrative structure of, 57–58; creation of, 19; federal lands transfer to, 35–36; Forest Service role in, 51–52; grasslands management and, 6–7. *See also* Black Hills National Forest; Federal Land Policy and Management Act of 1976; Klamath National Forest; Medicine Bow National Forest; Multiple Use–Sustained Yield Act

of 1960; Nebraska National Forest;
    Routt National Forest
National Grasslands Forum, 52–53
national grasslands trust fund, 126–30
National Grasslands Visitor Center,
    58, 80
National Industrial Recovery Act of
    1933, 29
national parks and monuments: land
    use planning in, 16. *See also* Bad-
    lands National Park; Grasslands
    National Park of Canada; Theo-
    dore Roosevelt National Park
National Park Service, 28
National Register of Historic Places,
    60, 107
National Resources Board, 26
National Scenic Trail, 72
Native Americans. *See* Indian
    reservations
natural resources: land use policy
    and, 19–20; and mineral rights, 15,
    111; national grasslands and, 67,
    87–90; royalty income from, 6, 126.
    See also Black Kettle NG; Comanche
    NG; Grasslands National Park of
    Canada; Little Missouri NG; Lyn-
    don B. Johnson NG; Rita Blanca NG
Natural Resources Planning Board, 16
Nature Conservancy, 128
Nebraska: drought cycles in, 12; grass-
    lands management in, 130; land
    use policy in, 17; livestock industry
    in, 13; national grasslands of, 67;
    subsistence homesteads in, 33. *See
    also* Oglala National Grassland;
    Sand Hills
Nebraska National Forest, 80
Nelson, Thomas C., 129
New Deal: Great Plains transforma-
tion during, 5–6, 12; land use poli-
    cies, 16, 18–19; land use reforms,
    25; post-war politics and, 49–50;
    resettlement experiments, 20–21;
    as social revolution, 118–20. *See
    also* Agricultural Adjustment Act
    of 1933
New Mexico. *See* Kiowa National
    Grassland
Norbeck, Peter, 21
North Country Trail, 72
North Dakota: livestock industry,
    13; subsistence homesteads in,
    33. *See also* Cedar River National
    Grassland; Little Missouri National
    Grassland; Sheyenne River Na-
    tional Grassland
Northern Great Plains: grasslands in,
    67–91
Northern Plains Conservation Net-
    work, 126–27

O'Brien, Dan, 84, 118
Ocean of Grass conservation assess-
    ment, 126–27
Ochoco National Forest, 57
Ogallala Aquifer, 101
Oglala National Grassland (Ne-
    braska), 84–87; archaeological sites
    in, 86; blocking up, 80; conserva-
    tion assessment of, 127; as L-U
    project, 37–44; map of, 85; tourism
    in, 84–86
oil and gas exploration. *See* energy
    resources; natural resources
Oklahoma, 91–92. *See also* Black
    Kettle National Grassland; Rita
    Blanca National Grassland
Oregon: L-U projects, 47–48. *See also*
    Crooked River National Grassland
overgrazing: grasslands depletion
    and, 13–15; grasslands management
    of, 40, 118; invasive plant species
    from, 53; mixed prairie domination
    from, 46; politics and, 72; wartime
    demands and, 49

parks. *See* national parks and monu-
    ments; state parks and recreation
    areas
Pawnee National Grassland (Colo-
    rado), 92–94; birdwatching in, 92;
    grazing allotments in, 93; historic
    landmarks in, 94; map of, 93; recre-
    ational uses in, 94
Perry, Bill, 81, 121
Peters, Tom, 96
Peterson, Mary, 88
Pettipiece, Gerry, 43
Pettipiece, Wes, 43
Picket Wire Canyonlands, 95–96
Pine Ridge Escarpment, 38, 84, 92
Pine Ridge Indian Reservation (South
    Dakota), 80–81, 127, 132
Pine Ridge L-U project, 37–38, 42
Pittman, Benjamin F., 40–41
politics: and grasslands management,
    49–51, 72, 122–23; and mineral
    rights, 111; New Deal reforms
    and, 25
Popper, Deborah, 119
Popper, Frank, 119
poverty, rural, 25, 37–38
Powell, John Wesley, 18
prairie dogs, 76, 82, 96, 112, 119–20, 122,
    124–27, 131–33
prescribed burns. *See* burns,
    controlled
Public Land Council, 122
public lands: American history and,

17–18, 60; dryland farming on, 15; grasslands depletion on, 14–15; grasslands management on, 6–7, 48–50; homestead vs. ranching struggle on, 13; land use planning for, 15–16; multiple use philosophy for, 50, 121; private grazing on, 123–25; private ownership of, 49–51; resource management on, 52. *See also* Federal Land Policy and Management Act of 1976

Public Rangelands Improvement Act of 1978, 51

Public Works Administration, 28

Quammen, O. S., 76

Ramsey, Bruce, 87–88
ranching, 12–13, 16. *See also* livestock industry
Read, Pete, 52
reclamation, 15–16, 20–22
recreational uses: grasslands management and, 6–7; increased grasslands use for, 60, 72, 107; multiple use programs and, 125; New Deal l-u projects for, 26; Resettlement Administration and, 32–35; submarginal lands for, 20;. *See also* Black Kettle NG; Cimarron NG; Grand River NG; Grasslands National Park of Canada; Little Missouri NG; Lyndon B. Johnson NG; McClellan Creek NG; Pawnee NG; Rita Blanca NG; Thunder Basin NG; tourism
Reichert, Randy, 9
reseeding management: environmental impact statements in, 50–51; invasive species and, 53; scs

rehabilitation by, 48. *See also* Cedar River NG; Cimarron NG; Curlew NG
Resettlement Administration (RA): federal relief efforts of, 30–35; and land purchase programs, 38–40; Nebraska project sites of, 39–40; resettlement experiments by, 20–21; Texas project sites of, 107
resettlement programs: cooperative farming sites in, 39–40; land appraisals in, 40–42; Resettlement Administration and, 30–35; subsistence homesteads, 25, 29–30. *See also* Bankhead-Jones Farm Tenant Act of 1937
resource management (multiple-use), 49–52, 121–23
riparian management, 54, 86, 97, 118
Rita Blanca National Grassland (Oklahoma, Texas), 99–101; blocking up, 99–100; grazing allotments in, 100; grazing permits in, 101; map of, 100; natural resources in, 100–101; recreational uses in, 101
Robel poles, 69, 76
Rockefeller, John D., 20
Rocky Mountains, 1–4, 11–12, 45, 92
Roosevelt, Eleanor, 25
Roosevelt, Franklin D., 5–6, 14, 21, 23–24
Roosevelt, Theodore, 19, 66–69
Routt National Forest, 91
Rowley, William D., 48
royalty income: Canadian grasslands and, 113–14; grasslands and, 6–7; 67, 126; natural resources and, 87, 111
rural life: Buffalo Commons concept and, 119–20; Jeffersonian agrarian philosophy and, 25; New Deal reforms for, 21–22; poverty and,

25, 37–38; subsistence homesteads program and, 29–30
rural rehabilitation, 30–35

sagebrush, 52–53, 60, 62, 65
sage grouse (sage hens), 53–54, 57, 62
Sand Hills (Nebraska), 1–2, 13
Santa Fe Trail, 91, 96–98, 103
Sather, Rod, 80
Sheldon, Addison E.: *Land Systems and Land Policies in Nebraska*, 17
Sheyenne River National Grassland (North Dakota), 70–73; controlled burns in, 72; exploring, 137–38; grazing allotments in, 72; land use alternatives in, 129–30; map of, 71; tourism in, 72
Shining Mountains. *See* Rocky Mountains
shortgrass prairie, 45–47. *See also* grass species
Skjoldal, Nate, 122
Smeltzer, Tom, 104
soil conservation: land repurchase for, 26–30; land use planning and, 16; Resettlement Administration and, 30–35. *See also* U.S. Department of Agriculture (USDA)
soil conservation districts, 42–44, 47
Soil Conversation Service, 31, 33, 35, 47, 121
Soil Erosion Service, 30–31
South Dakota: grasslands management in, 130; land use experiments in, 20–21; livestock industry in, 13; national grasslands in, 67; subsistence homesteads in, 33. *See also* Buffalo Gap NG; Custer State Park; Fort Pierre NG; Grand River

NG; Intertribal Bison Cooperative; National Grasslands Visitor Center

South Dakota Grasslanders Association, 84

Southern Great Plains: grasslands in, 91–111

species succession, 46–48

Sprentall, Bob, 87

Standing Rock Reservation, 73–75, 128–29

state parks and recreation areas: land purchase programs for, 38. *See also* Angastura Reservoir; Custer State Park; Fort Robinson State Park; Sully Creek State Park; Wood Mountain Regional Park

Sternsher, Bernard, 34

stewardship programs, 51

Stone, James C., 16

Stout, Jim, 65

submarginal lands: future alternatives for, 120–30; land use policy for, 19–21; land values of, 40–42; New Deal reforms and, 6, 25–30; Resettlement Administration and, 30–35; settlement and farming of, 13–16. *See also* Bankhead-Jones Farm Tenant Act of 1937; Taylor Grazing Act of 1934

subsidies and transfer payments, 119–20

subsistence homesteads program, 25, 28–30, 33–35

suburban resettlement, 30–35

Sugarloaf Grazing Association, 43–44, 87, 128

Sugarloaf Soil Conservation District, 42–44

Sully Creek State Park (North Dakota), 67

Sutton, Tyler, 127

tallgrass prairies, 2, 4, 45–47, 70–72, 130. *See also* grass species

Taylor Grazing Act of 1934, 16, 30, 123

tenant-rehabilitation programs, 20–21

Texas: longhorn cattle industry in, 12–13; national grasslands in, 91–92. *See also* Black Kettle NG; Caddo NG; Lyndon B. Johnson NG; McClellan Creek NG; Rita Blanca NG

Theodore Roosevelt National Park, 66–69, 129–30

Thunder Basin National Grassland (Wyoming), 87–91; black-footed ferret reintroduction in, 120; conservation assessment of, 126–27; map of, 87–91; recreational uses at, 90–91

timber resources, 7, 18–20

Timothy, Ken, 62

Toadstool Geologic Park, 85–86

tourism: grasslands management and, 7, 123–30; at Medora ND, 67, 70. *See also* Buffalo Gap NG; Caddo NG; Crooked River NG; Curlew NG; Grasslands National Park of Canada; Little Missouri NG; Oglala NG; recreational uses; Sheyenne River NG

Tugwell, Rexford G. "Rex the Red," 24–25, 30–35

Turner, Ted, 79

Turner Endangered Species Fund, 79

unappropriated land, 15, 30

U.S. Bureau of Agricultural Economics (BAE), 19–20, 24

U.S. Bureau of Biological Survey, 28

U.S. Bureau of Indian Affairs (BIA), 28

U.S. Bureau of Land Management (BLM): federal lands transfer to, 35–36; Forest Service cooperation with, 50; grasslands management by, 122. *See also* Taylor Grazing Act of 1934

U.S. Bureau of Reclamation, 123

USDA Agricultural Yearbook of 1923, 19–20

U.S. Department of Agriculture (USDA): and Bureau of Agricultural Economics, 19; land repurchase programs and, 27–30, 123–25; national grasslands and, 6; New Deal reforms and, 24–25; western range depletion and, 14–15. *See also* Farm Security Administration; Soil Conversation Service; Soil Erosion Service

U.S. Department of Justice, 28, 30

U.S. Department of the Interior: land repurchase programs and, 27; land use experiments and, 21–22. *See also* Soil Erosion Service; subsistence homesteads program

U.S. Forest Service: administrative structure of, 57–58; endangered species reintroduction by, 79; grasslands transfer to, 14–15, 35–36, 47, 51–52; grazing permits and, 43–44; land use alternatives of, 120–30; land use planning and, 16; management philosophy of, 48–50; national grasslands and, 6. *See also* Toadstool Geologic Park

U.S. General Land Office, 15

U.S. Geographical Survey, 18

U.S. government: land ownership and, 15–16, 49–51; land use policies of, 17–20; subsidies and transfer

payments by, 119–20. *See also*
Agricultural Adjustment Act of
1933; Bankhead-Jones Farm Tenant
Act of 1937; Emergency Relief
Act of 1935; Endangered Species
Act of 1973; Federal Land Policy
and Management Act of 1976;
Multiple Use–Sustained Yield Act
of 1960; National Environmental
Protection Act of 1969; National
Industrial Recovery Act of 1933;
Public Rangelands Improvement
Act of 1978; Taylor Grazing Act of
1934; Wilderness Act of 1964

VanBebber, Rick, 62
vegetational succession, 45–47

Wallace, Henry A., 14, 24
Wallace, Henry C., 14, 24
Walls, Nancy, 99, 103
water rights, 18–19
Weaver, John E., 13, 46–47
weeds: control of invasive species,
52–54, 77; "cool burns" control of,
60, 62; as cover crops, 48
Wilderness Act of 1964, 51
wilderness areas: grasslands as, 21,
84, 120
wild fires, 69, 86–87
Wild Idea Buffalo Company, 84
wildlife. *See* animals
wildlife preservation: environmental
impact statements in, 50–51; future
alternatives for, 123–30; grasslands
management and, 6–7, 53–54, 57;
land use planning and, 16; multiple
use programs and, 125; New Deal
L-U projects and, 26, 49; reseeding
management for, 62; Resettlement Administration and, 32–35;
submarginal lands for, 20. *See also*
Bankhead-Jones Farm Tenant
Act of 1937; animals; endangered
species
Wilson, E. P., 39
Wilson, M. L., 20, 29
Wisconsin glacier, 45
withdrawn land, 15, 30
Wood Mountain Regional Park
(Saskatchewan), 112–13
Works Progress Administration
(WPA), 33–34, 36
World War I, 13–14
World War II, 24, 49
Worster, Donald, 14
Wyoming: grasslands management in,
130; livestock industry, 13; national
grasslands in, 67. *See also* Thunder
Basin NG